FAITH IN THE MEDIA

FAITH IN THE MEDIA

A Christian critique of media values

Martin Field

Hodder & Stoughton
LONDON SYDNEY AUCKLAND TORONTO

British Library Cataloguing in Publication Data

Field, Martin
  Faith in the media.
  1. Mass media – Christian viewpoints
  I. Title
  261.52

  ISBN 0-340-54055-9

Published by Hodder and Stoughton, a division of Hodder and Stoughton Ltd, Mill Road, Dunton Green, Sevenoaks, Kent TN13 2AY.
Editorial Office: 47 Bedford Square, London WC1B 3DP.

Photoset by Chippendale Type Ltd, Otley, West Yorkshire.

Printed in Great Britain by Clays Ltd, St Ives plc.

To Bunny,
whose love, support and indulgence
never cease to amaze me!

Acknowledgements

With many thanks to all the staff at the Centre for Mass Communication Research, University of Leicester, for sharing with me their knowledge, insight and experience: Olga Linné, Graham Murdock, Anders Hansen and David Field for their support, encouragement and criticism of my work; the children at Hill House, Southwell, for their attempts to keep my feet on the ground and eyes off the television; and especially to the late Canon John Poulton for sharing his vision that the Church should discover new ways to communicate and express the love of God effectively in the modern world.

CONTENTS

Chapter One

Unlike the Elephant

There were six blind people. They heard that the king was visiting the next village, riding on an elephant. None of them had ever seen an elephant. 'An elephant!' they said. 'I wonder what an elephant is like.'

They went to find out. Each of them went alone. The first held the elephant's trunk. The second, a tusk. The third, an ear. The fourth, a leg. The fifth, the stomach. The sixth, the tail. Then they went home, all sure that they knew exactly what the elephant looked like.

They began to tell each other. 'Oh it's a fantastic elephant,' said the first, 'so slow and soft, long and strong.' 'No,' said the one who had felt the tusk. 'It's quite short, and very hard.' 'You are all wrong,' said the third, who had felt the ear. 'The elephant is flat and thin like a big leaf.' 'Oh no,' said the fourth, who had felt the leg. 'It's like a tree.'

And the other two joined in too: 'It's just like a wall,' 'It's like a rope.' They argued and argued, and their argument grew very bitter. They began to fight.

Then someone came up who could see. 'None of you is completely right,' he said. 'You need to understand how all the parts fit together to know what the elephant is like.'

The mass media – television, radio and the printed word – have become one of the most dominating features of contemporary society. They are our main source of entertainment, they tell us what's going on, what the weather will be like, which clothes to wear, which things to buy. They are multi-national, multi-million-pound businesses whose products we buy, whose images we consume and on which we have come to depend.

Christians cannot ignore them. They are full of stories about the Church – about who will be the next Archbishop, about homosexual clergy, about the latest attack on government policy, or the ignominious extra-marital exploits of a vicar from Surrey. They are becoming an increasing feature of Church life, with calls for the Churches to advertise and devote more money and resources to public relations.[1] Although fewer people attend church, more than sixty per cent of the British population tune in to radio and television religion. Religious broadcasts may be the closest many people ever get to the Gospel.

But our dependence on the media and the way the Church is beginning to 'use' them to proclaim the Gospel raise important questions.

Have they become a blessing or a curse? How do they influence our attitudes and behaviour? What effect do they have on everyday life? Do they pose a threat to traditional Christian values? Have they become the principal means of social control? Does it matter who owns them or how they are structured? Do they need firm regulation or a 'light touch'? Is religious television the most cost-effective way to proclaim the Gospel today (as one American broadcaster claims)? Is it leading us to develop new forms of religious expression, or does it represent a fatal accommodation to the spirit of the age? Can new technology be used to 'serve the common good' or will it simply reproduce traditional social inequalities and injustices? Are Christians right to preoccupy themselves with sex, violence and bad language? Or are they unwittingly diverting attention from more important pressing issues? What are the key issues and problems with which the media confront us and how does the Gospel relate to them?

Behind these questions lie two more fundamental ones.

First, what sort of a creature is the media 'elephant'? How are we to understand and describe it? Second, what are the Christian principles and values on which we can draw to guide our response to the elephant and how it can be used in today's world?

Powers, Tools and Social Forces . . .

In his book *God in a Box*, Colin Morris suggests that television is one of 'the most powerful of the principalities and powers – those secular institutions which are not under the Church's thumb but still within the range of God's sovereignty. It is by wrestling with principalities and powers that Christians achieve true spiritual maturity.'[2] Few can doubt the power of today's mass media. But they do not have an independent, autonomous life of their own. They are, inter alia, man made. Their pages and images are the end product of a complicated manufacturing process, coloured as much by economic, political and social forces as by creative and artistic ones. Their capacity to influence our thoughts and imagination is also mitigated by the circumstances in which we read and absorb them – they are part of our everyday lives. It is possible to be captivated by them with dire consequences.

Others claim that they are neutral tools. That although they can be used to dominate, exploit and control, they can also be used to liberate, enable and inform. They point to literacy campaigns in Latin America, 'Band Aid' in Britain and press campaigns of the 'fourth estate' as examples of the way in which the media can be used as a force for good in the world. The potential is there. They can be used for good or ill as we think fit. In today's television world, General Booth's question 'Why should the Devil have all the best tunes?' has become 'Why should Mammon have all the best shows?' as evangelical groups with their own TV stations emulate and compete with their secular counterparts.

But TV shows are not neutral. Their final content and form are determined as much by the politics and economics of production as they are by artistic and creative talent. It is, at best, fanciful and, at worst, a self-deception to assume that one can become a part of the television system and at the same time remain aloof from the values and forces which shape it. It is no accident that US religious programmes reflect the same acquisitive, privatised, individual and largely right-wing norms as the TV society in which they are set! Unlike the satellites which carry their messages, television programmes do not float in an ethereal vacuum. They are *programmes* – the end result of a complex, technical and commercial production system.

This institutional context of production, the latent cultural symbolism contained in media images and 'texts', the way audiences perceive them, and the wider context in which communication takes place mean that in order to understand the mass media we have to see them in a much wider social context.

They are neither neutral nor demonic. They are human institutions, created, regulated and operated by society. In wrestling with them, we are not wrestling with external powers – we are wrestling with ourselves.

Christian Principles

If we can only make sense of the media by seeing them as a feature of modern social life, then a Christian understanding of men and women and their place in society must be the starting point in developing a Christian response.

First, Christians share with others responsibility for the world. The fate of people and their world is inextricably linked – we are, as the Bible affirms and modern science explains, made of the same stuff! The recent interest in ecology and the well being of our planet has highlighted the fact that our fates are interdependent. In Manila at the first international gathering of Christian Communicators in

October, 1989, George Gerbner called for a new environmental movement which would also be concerned with cultural policies.[3] Just as the physical environment is essential to survival, the cultural environment is essential to the quality of that survival. Concern for the natural environment must embrace the cultural environment. A Christian concern for the world in which we live naturally extends to the media world.

Second, the Bible makes it plain that people are social beings – we share responsibility for each other. Many of the Old Testament laws relate to how the Israelites are to conduct their social affairs for the well being of all – particularly those in need of protection. Praiseworthy qualities are often 'interactive' ones. The Greek word *agapē*, usually translated as 'love' in the New Testament, is essentially a relational virtue, not an emotional feeling – borne out in deeds. St John's test of discipleship is that Christians should behave in a loving way to one another. Our relationship to God is discovered and realised in a social context.[4] Christians will be concerned about the role the media play in ordering our world, the way they shape our social values and relations, about how they encourage or inhibit viewers and listeners to play a full part in social life.

Third, communication is an essential part of God's world. Humankind not only has the potential to understand a God who communicates with and is recognised through his world, but as women and men created in his likeness, they also have the potential for that communication. We are not simply recipients of God's grace – we have the potential to share that grace with others. Created in the image of God, men and women are themselves creators – not simply consumers – in the field of communication as in any other. The UN MacBride Report talks about people's rights, not only to have access to the media, but to communicate with others for themselves. The Bible affirms that the need, desire and ability to communicate is an essential part of being human and of sharing in God's love.

Christian Responsibility

Our responsibility to God, for each other and for our world must therefore embrace a concern for the media – and display the same guiding principles and critical faculties that we bring to other features of social life – education, medicine, commerce etc. We must look beyond simple intention and ask deeper, more fundamental questions about the way that the media contribute to human life and examine the part they play in the light of a Christian understanding of God's plans for humankind.

The aims of those who would 'use' the media to win souls for Christ, for example, may be laudable. The danger is that they may adopt patterns of communication which instead of liberating people and giving them dignity as human beings created in the image of God, exploit, demean and devalue them. Advertising God may appear more worthwhile than lager, cigarettes, or soap powder. But in a world where successful advertising exploits emotions such as envy, fear, guilt, self-satisfaction and social division – to advertise at all may compromise the very Gospel they are trying to proclaim.

If men and women are to be responsible for each other and the world they share, then they need accurate, balanced and accessible information. If news is biased, distorted and information is controlled in the interests of one competing social group, then our capacity for responsible action is imperilled. If the media are dominated by a world view which suggests that one participates in society principally through the consumption or private possession of services and goods, then it stands in sharp contrast with a Christian understanding in which all have an equal place and value in the world and participation is seen in terms of our relationships with God and each other.

The media confront us with ourselves. Any attempt at a Christian appreciation or evaluation of them will draw us to look more critically at the place and value that people have in today's complex society.

Through a Glass Darkly

In his book *Super Media*, Michael Real points to our as yet limited understanding of the media. 'Our window onto media is as yet blurred and smudgy, but we do see the outlines and some details of what is there. It is difficult for human understanding to do better than this in any form of complex or profound knowledge. We use our theories and research as a lens through which to comprehend and direct external reality. What understanding we can manage in this way of biology, history, life, and meaning, we must treasure and make the most of.'[5]

Like the blind men and the elephant – we have but a partial picture of what the media world is like. But, however imperfect and incomplete, forms and images are beginning to emerge. Over fifty years of detailed research on the media and our awareness of how Christians are called to share responsibility for the society in which they live can help us begin to find answers to some of the questions they raise and the problems they pose.

Chapter Two

Society and the Media

'The mass media system, with its special information and communication resources is embedded in virtually every corner of social life, whether it be conflict, change, control, or societal integration.'

S.J. Ball-Rokeach & M.G. Cantor[1]

'It is meaningless to discuss any social institution such as mass communications as though it operated in isolation, unconnected to other social processes.'

P. Golding[2]

'It is . . . slowly coming to be realised that the public media are social institutions and that the question to be asked is: "How media function with regard to society as a whole".'

C. Hamelink, 1975[3]

Media or Society? A Focus of Concern

The history of the modern mass media is sometimes seen as a special instance of the more general way in which technical innovations have been adopted by society; each new development in media technology supplanting the previous one. As writing gave way to the printing press, so books, newspapers and magazines became the most popular news and entertainment media. In the early years of the twentieth century, the mass-media leisure market was dominated by the cinema and radio. And now television seems to have taken over from all these and has emerged as the most competitively diffused mass medium, spreading like a common cold over the face of the whole world. Tomorrow – who knows? As video, computer, satellite and 'digital' telecommunications become more integrated, they may produce new patterns of media consumption and herald the dawn of a new media era. Already India has 'leapfrogged' into the twenty-first century, bypassing intermediate technologies by introducing a sophisticated satellite communication system. In the Third World, scattered community groups are sharing vital development and campaign information through computer links and electronic noticeboards.

But despite all appearances to the contrary, technology does not have an independent life of its own. The history of the media is not simply a history of technical innovation. It is rather a history of the ways in which society has generated, shaped, controlled and used its technology. And technology itself, far from responding to some sort of divine, evolutionary imperative, has developed in response to social, political, economic, and more recently, military demands.

The phenomenal growth of the popular press in nineteenth-century Britain, for example, was not simply the result of great technological advances in print technology. It was the product of a number of inter-related factors: greater literacy; the increasing power of the newspaper-reading class; interest in the contentious public issues of war and reform; the abolition of Stamp Duty (by which the government had sought to gag the radical press). These were then complemented by the economic development of mass production and consumption and the attendant need for manufacturers to advertise competing brands.

The British Broadcasting Company (the forerunner of the BBC) was originally formed by industrialists who were keen to promote sales of the components for radio receivers. It was transformed into a unique corporation operating under royal charter by a government anxious to avoid the cacophony of a commercial 'free-for-all' such as existed in America at the time. They wanted to ensure that a medium of such exclusive power was not subverted for commercial gain, but used in the 'public' good and run as a public service.

Britain and the rest of Europe have very different press traditions. Whereas most newspapers in Britain are controlled by multi-national conglomerates, Europe has a much more diverse, 'partisan' pattern of ownership: newspapers are controlled by different political parties and trades unions. They all employ similar newspaper technologies. What is different is the system of tax subsidy and state control of ownership.

The difference between American and British television is not essentially a difference in broadcast technology, but a difference in how similar technology is regulated and controlled (see chapter seven for example). The BBC was created, in part, as a reaction to the perceived havoc of unrestrained, American, commercial competition! Its commitment to serve the public interest by providing a balanced schedule of programmes which conform to public standards of decency and good taste is enshrined in its unique charter.

'Public service' broadcasting was to be in the service of the community as a whole – an ideal which was reflected in the regulations which governed the introduction of commercial television in Britain in the 'fifties. Advocates claimed that this firmly regulated public service duopoly meant that broadcasting was responsive to consumer demand, protected from the excesses of open commercial competition and reasonably independent from direct government control. For example, the statutory public service requirement of commercial local radio in Britain and its oversight by the IBA is not a technological necessity, but a requirement to ensure that, in the face of commercial pressure, local interest and input was maintained in fact as well as in name. Stations were even obliged to use a proportion of their advertising revenue to support local 'live' music, for example.

The media do not stand over and against society; they are part of it. The way that their images are 'produced' and 'consumed' is as much a social as it is a technical phenomenon. If we wish to understand how the mass media work, how their images are shaped and the influence that they have on people's lives, we shall have to look at them as features of wider society. If we wish to discover the many ways we 'use' and are 'used' by the media today, we shall need to look beyond the early researchers' simple '4W' formula: *who* says *what* to *whom* and with *what* effect. We shall need rather to locate the media in the social order of which they are a part, to look at how they relate to other 'principalities and powers' which influence our lives. We shall need also not only to look at the messages they give us, but also at the underlying structures, functions and ideologies which control those messages and which are imparted to us *through* the modern mass media.

The Answers You Get Depend upon the Question You Ask . . .

Early media research was prompted by strictly commercial considerations. Systematic research into the contents and effects of media is a much more recent development. Before television and radio were invented, advertisers and media organisations could assess their market penetration by simply counting up the numbers of books, newspapers, magazines or cinema tickets which were sold. Radio and TV were different. If you wanted to know what people were listening to or watching, you had to go and ask.

Today, the bulk of media research is still sponsored by advertisers and media organisations. It is still concerned largely with consumption patterns, attitudes and individual use.[4] Other research has been prompted by concern for specific issues. For example, in the 'fifties public concern about the effects of the new television service (especially on children and young people) led to a study which set children's use of the media in the context of family life, academic performance and other leisure activities.[5] The Churches' fear about the effects of widely available video films led to research which played no small part in generating parliamentary support for the 1984 Video Recordings Act (see chapter four).[6] Current research in Britain includes studies of the impact of computers on home life, the way alcohol is portrayed on television and levels and types of violence on television.

But simply responding to 'public concern' can also impose limits – both on the range of problems which are seen to be important enough to warrant investigation and also on the terms in which they can be addressed. The development of an academic tradition has enabled new avenues of concern to be investigated and led to a more sophisticated understanding of how individuals 'use' the media and their wider influence and effect upon society.

Omnipotence, Impotence or Legitimation?

Early ideas about the media suggested that they were extremely powerful in moulding and shaping popular opinion. This idea was based on two things. Firstly, the *fact* that a single message could be simultaneously transmitted to millions of people and second the *assumption* that these millions of people could be 'persuaded of almost anything and could even be controlled'. In the aftermath of the Second World War, people wondered whether the impressive Nazi propaganda machine was largely responsible for ordinary men and women supporting a fascist state which condemned millions of its fellow citizens to the gas chamber. There seemed to be countless examples of incidents which showed how easily the public could be led and how good the media were at leading them.

One of the best documented and most striking demonstrations of the media's seemingly awesome power came after Orson Welles's legendary radio dramatisation of H.G.

Wells's *The War of the Worlds*. Accounts of thousands fleeing New York after its simulated news bulletins have become part of modern media mythology.[7] The mass media were seen rather like social syringes – capable of injecting new ideas, ways of thinking and patterns of behaviour into an unresisting and unyielding society. Their effects were *personal*, *dramatic* and *immediate*.

The shortcomings of this rather simplistic 'hypodermic' theory were soon exposed. The notion that the media were omnipotent was dented by a British Labour landslide victory in the 1945 election in the face of over-riding press support for the Conservative Party, and also by American research which looked more closely at the way in which individuals 'used' the media. People were not isolated, anomic individuals but were members of families, social groups and communities. They were influenced by things other than the media – by education, by their friends and neighbours, by the Church, by their upbringing, by their everyday experiences and encounters. When the relationship between individual media consumption and behaviour and attitude was measured more finely, it appeared that many of these other influences were considerably stronger.

Now, studies looked at the way people responded to political campaigns, at the way in which farmers and doctors adopted innovations, at the different ways people reacted to and read the same media images. They seemed to suggest that media influence was much more complex, that it played a secondary role in determining behaviour, reinforcing patterns rather than determining them. In 1960 an influential review of research concluded that the mass media functioned 'through a nexus of mediating factors'. Research did not show that they were without effects, but established the *primacy* of other influences on behaviour. However, these new ideas and studies were harder for the public to grasp. Their research was much more specific and detailed and employed a wider range of more sophisticated methodologies. Popular fears continued to be fuelled by broadcasters, advertisers and dissenting researchers who clung to the more simple, dramatic and easily understood model of a direct link between the media and behaviour.

During the 'seventies and 'eighties, media research methods of investigation were refined. Sociology, economics and political science began to make their contribution to a developing academic field. International studies enabled researchers to compare media influence in different cultures and societies. The attention of mass communications research shifted from simply examining the short-term effects of purposive intent (campaigns, advertisements etc) to looking at long-term influences as well. Media policy, finance and control, the effect of advertising, how media organisations functioned, how their images were produced – all these were drawn into the investigative net. Researchers began to investigate more seriously the unintended 'side-effects' of media images, their social impact and the way they influenced public awareness.

They began to look at a whole new range of questions and concerns. Are the media guilty of outright distortion? Do their acceptance and transmission of conventional ways of doing things amount to a form of control? Are they agents of change, as many suppose, or do they inhibit change? Do they open up new areas of social investigation (the BBC drama *Cathy Come Home* highlighted the plight of the homeless)? Or are issues often presented out of context, as disconnected events without adequate background information? Do they contribute to the democratic process? Or does their inevitable dramatisation of social and political issues impair understanding and make intelligent decision-making harder?

Research looking at these sorts of questions exposed once more the potency, power and widespread influence of the media in modern consumer society. 'The social power of the media is once more at the centre of attention for some social scientists, a circumstance which is not the result of a mere change of fashion, but of a genuine advance of knowledge based on secure foundations.'[8] The immediate, dramatic link between media and behaviour has become far more tenuous. But the social processes are even harder for the uninitiated to grasp and their theoretical framework, more contentious.

Many people still cling to a much more easily grasped understanding of media power. They are determined not to be diverted by what they regard as spurious evidence and dubious facts produced by 'liberal' researchers. Rejecting the title of the Broadcasting Standards Council's research into the connection between television and behaviour – *A Measure of Uncertainty*[9] – one speaker at the Church of England's General Synod 15th February, 1990, debate on the influence of the media said: 'I don't care what anybody says. Nobody will convince me that children are not affected by it. Some are brutalised by it; they're getting anaesthetised by it.' And she concluded to loud applause: 'The sooner we do something about it the better!'[10]

Advertisers and the commercial and public media (which continue to sponsor most research) have a vested interest in perpetuating a 'traditional' model of media power. News organisations have reacted angrily to the accusations that their images may be unwittingly biased or partial and have sponsored research to challenge some of the more critical findings.[11] 'Belief in the persuasiveness of the media, in their moral impact, monopolisation of leisure and erosion of traditional pursuits, intellectual frivolousness and triviality has not only shaped the way the media behave, but has also had enormous impact on the questions addressed by critics and social scientists,' comments one prominent British researcher, bitterly. ' . . . Shoals of red herrings have nurtured a great deal of unimportant research, and uninformed criticism which hinder our understanding of the media in contemporary Britain.'[12]

Whilst critical and informed understanding has developed through careful analysis of contradictory and conflicting 'evidence', popular understanding is locked in a time warp. Drawing on traditional and outdated models of media influence which have, by and large, been superseded by more recent detailed research, Christian media campaigners have often seemed more adept at finding new ways to vocalise old fears, than they have in coming to terms with a more developed understanding of the role and function of the media in society.

Before we examine in greater detail four of the media 'issues' which raise particular concerns for Christians, it is worthwhile setting out some of the more general features of the modern mass media that research has uncovered.

Chapter Three

It's not what you do, it's the way you do it: The Power of the Media

'The media system links virtually all major parts of the society to one another, and is thus involved in virtually every major process of conflict, change, integrations, and control that power seekers, communities, states and whole societies must face.'

S.J. Ball-Rokeach and M.G. Cantor [1]

'Nobody can be sure about what television does to the viewer. One opinion holds that television programmes can subjugate whole populations and turn children into murderers. Another opinion holds that television is too trivial a cultural event to be considered. A surprising number of experts have subscribed to both these opinions in close succession or even simultaneously.'

Clive James [2]

' . . . from within their private crevices, people find themselves relying on the media for concepts, for images of their heroes, for guiding information, for emotional charges, for a recognition of public values, for symbols in general, even for language. Of all the institutions of daily life, the media specialise in orchestrating everyday consciousness – by virtue of their pervasiveness, their accessibility, their centralised symbolic capacity. They name the world's parts, they certify reality as reality . . . To put it simply the mass media have become core systems for the distribution of ideology.'

Todd Gitlin [3]

Public Concern

Times of rapid social change and technological innovation produce anxiety about traditional values and ways of life. The latest form of popular mass entertainment has always provided a scapegoat for such anxieties. The Viennese waltz was accused of corrupting social morals; music halls were said to incite drunkenness and crime; in the 'fifties, US 'adventure' comics were once claimed to encourage teen-age aggression; the cinema was blamed for the break-up of family life and leading its young audiences astray. In their time, both rock music and television have been accused of destroying family values and creative imagination, and inciting crime, violence and lust. In recent years, the 'video-nasty' containing combinations of violence and sex has donned this mantle of corruption – 'a mental and moral health hazard of a kind we have not experienced before'.[4] Fears have also been expressed about the pernicious and addictive influences of amusement arcades and computer video games.

Fears in Perspective

Although piling social ills onto a media scapegoat may be therapeutic for some, good 'copy' for newspapers and offer middle-class parents superficial accounts of where they went wrong, they distract attention from more serious and pertinent analyses. A more sober appraisal of evidence that has accumulated about the media allows us to set these fears in their wider context. It also alerts us to other more pertinent issues and sets out more pressing concerns.

1. The power to change your life?

Advertisements for Volvo cars project a safe, reliable, family image. A company which buys its employees a Volvo shows how much it cares about them. A man who transports his family in a Volvo shows how much he loves them. Indeed a Volvo which is also a sports car creates a new set of rules! Volvo adverts are primarily aimed at existing owners, reassuring them that they have made the right choice so that they will be sure to choose another Volvo next time round: they become evangelists for the marque.

Advertisers have come to realise that the media are much more successful at reinforcing values and beliefs than they are at changing them. Attempts to use the media to promote fundamental changes in attitudes and opinions have often failed. The failure of innovative (and expensive) media campaigns to persuade people to change their behaviour prompted health and development workers in the Third World to look again at what the mass media could and could not do. They found that discussion groups, personal contact and living example are the best ways to *introduce* change into society.

Similarly, high-profile media campaigns alerting people to the dangers of AIDS may have raised public awareness about the disease. But there is little evidence to suppose that they have been effective in changing everyday sexual practices and behaviour – particularly among those at greatest risk. Communication effects are greatest where messages are in line with existing opinions, beliefs and dispositions, where the aim is reinforcement rather than change. People look to the media for reassurance about behavioural changes they have already made.

Critics suggest that one of the most disturbing and subtle side-effects of media dominated by consumer advertisements is the way in which they endorse the view that the private possession of material goods brings happiness and confers status (see chapter five). Populist critics argue that media moguls have the power to change and mould society. The anecdotal evidence they frequently offer (of children's playground games and copy-cat crimes) is more illustrative than explanatory and usually ignores the overwhelming fact that the behaviour of most viewers and listeners is unaffected! Communications researchers, developing a more

sophisticated understanding of the way that the media reinforce attitudes and opinions, are once more beginning to
stress the power of media images. The evidence turns populist ideas upside-down. Far from being agents of change, the
mass media are much more effective in lending legitimacy
to the established order and current ways of doing things.

2. *Symbolic annihilation! – the media's great disappearing
   trick!*

Like cartoons, television deals in stereotypes. It is in
its nature to do so. However, studies of media content
have shown that certain groups are systematically *under-*
represented in all media, whilst others are consistently
*mis-*represented. One critic called the combined effect
of this 'symbolic annihilation'. For example, women are
significantly under-represented in the media – particularly
on television. When they *are* portrayed it is often in a relationship which reinforces male dominance and authority.
Females are attractive adjuncts and decorations or provide
a useful context to reassert male power. Advertisements
provide some of the most glaring examples of this. Women
usually either provide seductive decoration, or are confined
to the role of willing, contented, household slave whose
prime concern is whether their washing smells, or the
number of germs lurking down the loo![5] Male supremacy
and authority is further reinforced by their near monopoly of
'voice-overs' (even when the products advertised are aimed
specifically at women!).

Apologists are quick to point out that the media can only
reflect reality. They suggest that in a world where men do
indeed hold positions of power and authority it would be unrealistic to expect the media to portray anything else. They
point to series such as *Juliet Bravo* and *Cagney and Lacey*
which offer alternative images and try to show women in
equivalent positions of power. But their arguments are far
from convincing. Often the appeal (and usually the bulk of
the story-line) of series in which women are in positions of

power lies in the way in which the situation is presented as unusual. Alternatively, female power is seen as a sexual adjunct; hemlines and bedroom scenes an integral part of the plot. And if the media really did reflect social reality their portrayal of working women, the elderly, blacks, gays etc would be much more frequent and representative than it is.

It is not only women who find that they have been abused by the media. Clergy are sometimes flattered by the comment: 'Surely *you're* not a vicar – you're different.' It may not be much of a compliment. Most clergy should indeed be very different from their media counterparts (the closest some people ever get to the Church!).[6] Groups which are already on the margins of society (oppositional political groups, racial and ethnic minorities, the handicapped, those who challenge social conventions, strikers, 'peace campaigners' and nowadays even Christians and churchgoers) either disappear completely from media view or conform to such distorted stereotypes that they (and their cause) are marginalised still further.[7] Whereas clergy often have an opportunity to confront, correct (or confirm) their public image in real life, many marginalised groups (who by definition are fewer in number) do not. During the 1985 miners' strike, mining communities became extremely upset and angry by their portrayal. Few people outside their communities understood or sympathised with the reasons which lay behind it. Public perception of events was almost invariably determined by the 'official' perspective which the media reflected (see chapter six).

3. . . . You in your small corner, and I in mine.

Media audiences are not made up of blank pieces of human blotting-paper helplessly soaking up anything that comes their way. They choose (from the very limited ranges available) *which* newspaper to buy, *which* books to read, *which* films to go and see. But a closer study of the *way* that audiences watch television or use the other media suggests that people are also highly selective in interpreting the media images they choose. The pre-conceived ideas that people bring with them when they watch television or read a newspaper helps them to select and 'filter' what they see. The same television programme or newspaper story can present different messages to different viewers. The media often simply serve to reinforce a firmly held opinion.

A study which looked at the way in which people watched a current affairs programme found that different social groups received very different messages. Groups which were dominated by a Conservative outlook (apprentices, teacher-training students and bank managers) tended to find their views of the world confirmed; those dominated by Labour or socialist discourses (shop stewards, trade-union officials, and a group of students) tended to challenge and question the views it presented. Black students found it largely irrelevant to their concerns.[8] A recent international comparison of *Dynasty* viewers found that males and females watched for different reasons and 'read' different lessons. Part of the widespread appeal of soap operas lies in the way that they offer their viewers kaleidoscopic, morality plays and allow them to identify with the various attitudes and behaviour of a succession of characters before coming to their own conclusions.[9] Should Michelle (from *EastEnders*) have an abortion or not? The reaction and opinions of the different television characters allow viewers to rehearse their own views and opinions.

News coverage of inner-city riots, too, may present different images to different audiences. For the rioters it suggests that violent insurrection may be one of the few means at their disposal to draw public attention to their grievances and problems. The police and wider public, on the other hand, may come to regard all inner cities as potential trouble-spots. 'Strong' policing in similar situations may precipitate the very problems that it is designed to prevent.

The selective picture of reality that the media offer is compounded still further by the way that audiences often seek out and interpret messages to reinforce pre-conceived views and opinions.

4. A dependency culture?

Marshall McCluhan coined the phrase 'global village' to describe a world which he claimed had been transformed by the mass media. The plight of the starving in Ethiopia, the tragic events in Tiananmen Square, the struggle of daily life in Beirut, the Palestinians in the Middle East, the blacks in South Africa have become our nightly concern. But the term global 'village' is not entirely appropriate. Our concerns *are* global – distance is no longer an object. But the village is a very strange one. Unlike a traditional community, we cannot possibly know all about the daily business and private lives of each of its millions of inhabitants. The media select for us a mere handful of its issues and concerns. They present them to us in their own inimitable way. The 'global village' is made up of people who hardly ever leave their huts and depend on professional story-tellers to tell them what the outside world is like.

Television is widely regarded as the most trustworthy of these story-tellers. What it says, goes. Although most people claim that it represents their main source of news about world events,[10] studies which have looked at the way in which people 'use' different media suggest that it is at least complemented by society's other story-tellers: the national press, local 'free' newspapers, national, local and commercial radio.[11] People test out their experience of the world, their views and opinions by comparing them with the information they receive through the media. Conscious selection is complemented by more unwitting absorption. News images are reinforced by the popular entertainment media. The values of late-Victorian imperialism were enshrined in the popular boys' fiction of the day. The social status, power and economic role of women today is similarly encapsulated in the images presented in journals, television programmes, advertisements and pulp fiction.

When information is scarce, when it is important, when people are anxious or confused (such as in wartime or in a crisis) they become even more dependent upon the media and turn to the media to help them resolve their dilemmas and problems, often preferring them to inter-personal information.[12] In December 1989, a revolution in Romania overthrew the dictatorship of President Ceausescu. With their government collapsing around their ears, the people of Romania turned to foreign news bulletins and impromptu news-sheets to find out what was happening in their own capital. When an earthquake hit San Francisco in September 1989, people tuned to TV and local radio to find out what was happening in their own city and street. As the mass media assume an ever-increasing role in defining and interpreting the events going on around us and our place within them, so we become more dependent upon them for our understanding of social reality.

5. Social glue

Watching television is essentially an 'individual' experience (TV presenters are taught to speak to a single viewer). At the same time, many millions of people share in the same 'private' event. Television is the epitome of western industrial democratic life. Our main leisure activity has become a common, shared experience of 'private' consumption.

Studies which have compared television content and the attitudes and opinions of viewers over a number of years have found that their perceptions are becoming closer to the view of the world that television promotes. People who spend more time watching television seem to be more affected by its stereotypical display of reality. They share its way of looking at the world. 'The mass media world view tells us that we are basically good, that happiness is the chief end of life, and that happiness consists in obtaining material goods . . . The media constrict our experience and substitute media world for real world so that we become less and less able to make the fine value-judgments that living in such a complex world requires.'[13]

A study which looked at racial attitudes of young people in Britain found that their perception of 'racial problems' was almost identical to the way they were portrayed by the media. Awareness of the prejudice, discrimination, and white hostility against coloured people, a concern with the number of coloured people entering the country, and the association of coloured people with riots and troubles were among the themes most closely associated with the media and were central to the press handling of race.[14] The social, psychological, political and historical roots of racism and racial prejudice receive little attention.

As more people depend on the mass media for an understanding of the world in which they live, so society gradually shares common, prevailing values and assumptions. This is at a much deeper level than is immediately apparent, given each person's superficially individual response. One commentator has called television 'the soul of the nation'.

6. Setting the public agenda

The media are faced with an almost infinite number of issues and events. They can only present a limited range of them. They set before the public a restricted agenda of important issues and problems. Sometimes this represents a conscious attempt by interested groups to 'mould' public opinion. The *Sunday Times* campaigned for compensation for the victims of the thalidomide drug. Bob Geldof made African famine a global issue. At election time, each political party tries to present *its* range of issues and personalities to the electorate. Since 1979, issues and policies have become part of a single, integrated advertising campaign. The democratic ideal in which voters are provided with the necessary information from which to make an informed political choice has been subverted by the modern 'media campaign'. A good television image is far more important than sensible, coherent policies. Both Labour and Conservative parties have professional media advice. Rallies, TV interviews and press conferences are stage-managed – right down to the choice of chair!

Much of the process of learning through the media is incidental, as unplanned and unconscious for the receiver as it is unintentional for the sender. Audiences and readers are presented with a consistent and coherent picture of social reality. They are offered a context in which they can understand their own place. The way the media cover a story, the range of issues that they address, even the language and pictures that they use are significant (if subtle) factors which help to create 'public opinion'. For example, Have the cameras or reporters concentrated on an isolated violent incident rather than the largely peaceful protest of which it was a part? Is it a 'strike', a 'dispute', 'protest action' or 'illegal secondary picketing'? Do we see pictures of people who are despondent, angry, upset or frustrated? Are policemen the only injured people we see? Are the bosses presented as relaxed, reasonable and self-assured, interviewed from within the safe confines of a comfortable office whilst union leaders are seen outside, their hair blowing about in the wind, surrounded by their members, responding off the cuff to impromptu questions? All these things can colour the way we see the participants in a dispute and whether we think it is 'right' or 'wrong'. Again, the media become the 'soul' of the nation.

The question, What do the media cause people to talk and think *about*? is being seen as a more subtle, although more important and meaningful question, than, What do the media cause people to think?

7. Ownership and a 'free market'

One of the ways in which the media can help people play a full role in society is by providing them with the information they need to do that. Some see the concentrated patterns of ownership and control within society as restrictive and claim that they inhibit the range of views and opinions upon which democracy depends.

Mass-media content is the end result of a complicated, industrialised production process. Its images are subject

to various levels of influence and control. Studies have
looked at the effects that these different influences have
on the images we read and receive. These studies do seem
to give cause for misgiving, as we will see.

At one level, mass-media content is clearly the product
of the people who actually *create* it – authors, producers,
script-writers, actors and journalists. But these people do
not create their work in splendid isolation. They are subject to higher authorities – editors and sub-editors, station
controllers, those who plan the evening's radio and television schedules. These 'media managers' often exercise
considerable influence when selecting which areas should
be covered, which departments will be given access to
organisational resources, which stories will be presented
on the front page, which titles will be added to a publisher's
list etc. But they, in turn, are subject to higher authorities
– owners, boards of management, advertisers, governing
bodies, statutory and regulatory authorities. Although these
people seem to be far removed from the final 'product',
they often exercise considerable influence over what is
produced. They do not often have to interfere directly
in the production process: things work their way in any
case. They simply decide which managers and editors to
appoint (or sack!), which part of the organisation should
receive a greater or lesser share of corporate resources, the
overall style and approach that a newspaper should adopt,
the 'market' at which it is aimed, etc. Those who write or
work for them usually know the limits within which they can
work, and the sort of acceptable products they can create.
When the owners of a major national newspaper recently
decided to compete 'down-market', some of its journalists
left, unable to share the outlook and images demanded by
its new editor.

Over the years media ownership and control in Britain
has become concentrated in fewer and fewer hands. Robert
Maxwell and Rupert Murdoch control between them the
lion's share of national newspaper circulation. Commercial local radio stations are beginning to amalgamate. The

commercial vulnerability of community radio – supposedly a local third tier of broadcasting – is making them vulnerable to predatory media groups. New journals and periodicals have to satisfy the demands of one of two major wholesalers if they are ever to reach the shelves of the local newsagent. At the same time, many of the traditional media have become part of larger groups through takeovers and amalgamations with companies who have similar or complementary interests. These companies have interests in newspapers, television, film and satellite. They control the production, and distribution of films, books, records, magazines and video games.

It comes as little surprise to learn that many of the newspapers whose editorials supported the government's contention that further 'de-regulation' rather than public investment was the best way to take advantage of new communications opportunities are themselves part of extensive international media empires and stand to gain most from such proposals. The joint processes of conglomeration and diversification mean that fewer people now exercise greater control over the production and distribution of a larger part of our media than ever before.[15] And media which are part of much larger national and international conglomerates – with commercial interests which extend into every sphere of consumer life – are unlikely to be harbingers of radical, or challenging, thoughts and ideas.

Others argue that ownership is unimportant, that in the competitive media world the 'consumer is king'. At the heart of the 1990 Broadcasting Act lies the whole notion of 'consumer sovereignty' – the public as the final arbiters of which cultural artifacts survive. But consumers can only choose from what is currently available. Commercial viability does not depend solely upon popular support. For example, the *Daily Herald* was read by more people than *The Times*, *Financial Times* and *Guardian* put together when it went under – but the sort of people who read it were not the sort advertisers wanted to reach. 1988 saw the launch of a new regional paper in Manchester. It failed, not because it was a poor product but because it failed to attract sufficient advertising revenue. Human need is not determined by profitability.

Some, whilst conceding that the press are partisan, and reflect the values and ideas of owners and advertisers, claim that the same does not apply to the broadcast media, which are responsible to public bodies. But they too compete for their share of the media audience – either to support their case for public funding, or to satisfy the demands of advertisers. They also try to appeal to as wide an audience as possible. They too are part of the popular 'mainstream' and operate within the same 'consensus-band' as most newspapers, and draw on the social values and assumptions which are most widely legitimated. This makes it extremely hard for any of the popular mass media either to present the needs and interests of minority social groups, or to reflect diverse views and opinions. 'Although it has been manifest to everybody that political, social, economic and cultural interests, values and opinions have appeared to become more and more disparate, and this disparity more and more organised, the kind of opinions and attitudes and values and above all information conveyed by broadcasting and the press has tended to become more constrained and more internally consistent.'[16]

The government rightly claim that competition has led to more newspapers and journals than ever before, but a range of titles is not the same as a range of opinions. Private ownership and competition seem unable to provide media which adequately reflect the diverse views and opinions necessary to a healthy society. They represent a movement away from the protection of public interests and towards the promotion of corporate ones.

8. A threat to family life?

The mass media (and television in particular) have often been accused of contributing to the demise of family life. Although there is little evidence to support it, they have often been blamed for introducing values inimical to it. If we look instead at the way that families use the media (and one recent piece of research has done just that – by putting a video camera inside a TV set and filming families watching 'the box') we find that the media have a rather different role. They are often the focus of social activity – families watch favourite programmes together, they discuss which programme to watch or 'who's done what' when someone was out of the room. People go to the cinema with their friends, they discuss at work what they've read in the paper or seen on television the night before. The media provide opportunities for families to assert role models and values – children are denied access to certain books, comics and TV programmes by their parents, they are made to listen to 'their music' on their own cassette players; fathers dominate the use of the TV remote control, often taking it with them when they leave the room!

Whilst some have also accused the media of contributing to family tension by providing members with new role models, attitudes and patterns of behaviour, most research suggests that these are rather learned *outside* the home. Instead, the media provide irate parents with further examples of the same behaviour. They become convenient scapegoats. A preoccupation with the way that media content affects the behaviour and attitudes of families may divert attention from other influences; for example, their importance in family economic activity.

The media are significant areas of family expenditure. Most families own (or rent) a range of technical equipment – satellite dishes, TV sets, video recorders, compact disc, tape and record players. They also purchase and consume a number of media 'products' – newspapers, magazines, records and compact discs, cinema and theatre tickets. They may pay a satellite subscription, and almost certainly pay a BBC licence fee and support commercial television through the unseen (although considerable) 'advertisement levy' on all household purchases. As the home becomes an increasing focus of leisure activities, and leisure becomes further commodified, media expenditure is likely to represent an increasing proportion of the family budget. Today's media world already includes laser discs, satellite dishes, subscriptions for additional TV channels, digital tape recorders and an increased use of computer-controlled telecommunications resources (Prestel, Viewdata, electronic mail, etc). Social and commercial pressure urges us to keep up with these latest technologies, to give our children the same opportunities that others have, to buy into privatised entertainment media and leisure activities as public-service ones decline.

Second, the increase in advertising necessary to sustain these new media outlets and their portrayal of increasingly affluent lifestyles will also exert pressure on family budgets. Many parents are already concerned at the level of advertising directed to children at Christmas. Pressure to 'keep up with the Joneses' is nothing new, but these days it is no longer the family next door who provide children with their material goal, but Jones Inc. – the international toy conglomerate who is able to saturate the media with the message that his products are *essential* for a Happy Christmas. It is becoming harder to tell the difference between advertisements and the programmes themselves.

The family is not only a social unit, it is also an economic one. As such, it is of more than passing interest to media which reflect increasingly commercial objectives.

9. Nation shall speak unto nation

The media are international big business. First, their products are sold from one country to another. *Dallas*, *Dynasty*, *Starsky and Hutch* are as internationally available as Coca-Cola. Britain is an importer and exporter of television programmes. *To the Manor Born* is as popular in India as it was in Britain! But the economics of production means that there is a net flow from the developed western countries to the Third World. Most of the initial production cost is retrieved in domestic transmission. Anything that can be realised in international sales is icing on the cake. Programmes are 'dumped' on the Third World. It is far cheaper for them to buy in lavish western productions than to produce their own programmes from scratch. Television in the Third World is swamped with western images and values. Even locally produced programmes reproduce the western formats, styles and images that audiences have come to expect.

Second, information goods (such as news items) are of great social significance. Four western news agencies dominate 'world news'. Domestic news media in Third World countries have greater access to news and images of the developed world than they do to events in their own countries! Much of the information may be irrelevant or even damaging to local culture and autonomy. It preserves and enhances the view that what goes on in Washington, London and Moscow is of far more importance than what is happening in neighbouring states. In the face of such ideological dominance, UNESCO argued that information should not only be freely available, but should be 'balanced' as well.[17]

Third, media ownership is truly trans-national. In developing and Third World countries, media ownership usually reflects and perpetuates traditional colonial patterns of dependence. Educational publications in Anglophone Africa are almost always printed in English by British-owned companies. Theological books are often translated from British or American originals and reflect largely western concerns and insights. Imported values and ideas dominate the Third World ideological arena. Western governments often express concern and legislate to prevent important domestic industries falling into foreign control. They rarely display the same concern about their domination of Third World interests.

Fourth, the emerging media are intrinsically international. Satellite communications transcend national boundaries. Once again, although seemingly internationally regulated through INTELSAT, these are dominated by the west. Twenty-three per cent of non-military satellites are controlled by the United States. Many of these are dedicated to private use – ensuring that those who already exercise the most economic power (and can therefore afford to deploy such expensive technology) will maintain their advantage. Those that will provide entertainment and news are increasingly controlled by multi-national commercial organisations (Rupert Murdoch's Sky channel already broadcasts to most of western Europe) and pose a further threat to national control of communications. They also pose a commercial threat to existing national networks.

The economic and political dominance of the Third World by the west is supplemented and enhanced by cultural and media imperialism. Media content, ownership and technology all reflect western dominance and serve to reinforce dependent relationships. Under the guise of a free flow of information and technology, western nations are underpinning their global dominance and contributing to continued third-world underdevelopment.

10. Technology and the future

Technology is made up of two essential components:

a) *the technique* – the equipment and expertise necessary to use it.
b) *the social organisation* – the structure and ideology which determine how society utilises 'the technique'.[18]

Television, for example, is a complicated communications technique which produces electronic images. It requires a high level of expertise to design, manufacture and operate its expensive equipment. But the term 'television' also refers to the social system in which electronic images are produced, transmitted, and received. When the British proudly claim to have the 'least worst television in the world', they are not referring to British television equipment or studio 'expertise', but to the way in which both have been utilised to produce a certain type and quality of programme.

Neil Postman suggests that America is 'amusing itself to death'.[19] He argues that television presents information in a form that renders it 'simplistic, non-substantive, non-historical, and non-contextual'. Information is packaged as entertainment. It has become the ultimate 'trivial pursuit'. But like many of those who see new technology as one of the principal determinants of social change, his trenchant criticism of the way that American society has become dominated by television is less a critique of the 'technique' (the electronic gadgetry) and more a comment on the way that it has been deployed and developed in America. The values that television promotes are the values of the society in which it exists. He goes along with Colin Morris's suggestion that television is one of the world's 'principalities and powers' – that the 'technique' itself is neutral. It can be employed for good or ill as society determines. Television's power comes not from its tubes and transistors, but from its place in society.

Those who look either gloomily or optimistically to a technology-led future must draw an important distinction between the techniques that will be available and the ways in which society will choose to deploy them and whose interests they will serve. For example, many have pointed to the advantages of home shopping. By using a television set, a computer, and an ordinary telephone it is already possible for people to order their groceries from home. Such a system could be a boon to those who are ill, elderly, handicapped or housebound. But the technology will only be available to those with sufficient resources to purchase the equipment themselves.

The equipment is beyond the reach of those who form some of the poorest sections of society and need it most. It would be of greatest benefit to those who live in isolated rural communities, and are either unable – or often cannot afford – to travel to urban centres. But it is only currently available in London and other large cities as a luxury convenience at prices which reflect the high cost of delivery.

India tried to bridge the social gap – with an ambitious project which sought to use satellite television to bring educational resources to otherwise inaccessible rural communities. Many villages were provided with a communal television set. Entertaining programmes were produced to help villagers learn about new agricultural developments, to improve basic health care, to help rural teachers gain access to further 'in-service' training. But satellite channels are expensive to develop and maintain and the system soon came under pressure to use some of its spare capacity for commercial services. The national and international advertisers who were willing to underwrite some of the costs involved wanted to reach the richer, higher-spending, urban élites who lived in the cities. Soon the same satellite channels were used to carry entertainment programmes like *To the Manor Born* and *I Love Lucy* and advertisements for soap, shampoo and soft drinks. As a result, once the new communication channels carried these images as well, far from strengthening local village life, they simply added further pressures and frustrations, offering images and products of a world beyond the grasp of village viewers.

New computer and communication technologies have made more information more accessible than ever before and, in theory, more information makes it possible to share solutions to common problems, to learn from other people's mistakes, and create a more just and equitable social order. But that would only be if everyone had access to this information which – as critics have pointed out – is not the case. The gap between rich and poor is matched by an increasing gap between the 'information rich' and the 'information poor'. In Britain, the withering of public information and leisure provision is coupled with a tendency to charge for remaining services. Access to them is increasingly a function of ability to pay. As social inequalities in Britain intensify the less well off become disadvantaged twice over. They cannot afford the newly commercialised services and the increasingly impoverished public institutions are unable to provide them.[20] The poor are doubly disadvantaged.

At an international level, the situation is even more aggravated. One analyst comments that 'given the prevailing structure of global industrial and military power, it is difficult to believe that the communications revolution is not the outcome of deliberate and extensive efforts to maintain a worldwide system of economic advantage.'[21] For example, using advanced photographic techniques, surveillance satellites are now able to provide early information about crop diseases in many parts of the Third World. But this vital information is private. It is available for purchase. It needs to be analysed by experts. Important early information about plant disease in commodities such as coffee (a vital cash crop to many Third World economies), is used by western banks and commodity brokers to adjust their future purchasing strategy, instead of enabling producers to improve their crops and standard of living.

Democracy is founded upon the principle of an informed electorate making responsible choices and decisions. The mass media are key elements in providing that information, and often determine what is available in the public domain. However, new technology which has the potential to make information more widely available and more equitably shared is largely being developed and dominated by private interests for commercial gain. The capacity of the average citizen to make informed and responsible judgments is thus significantly imperilled and reduced. Real information is becoming scarce. Entertaining trivia abounds.

The Real Challenge of the New Democracy

What many critics are still most concerned about are the short-term effects of media content. Support for the 1984 Video Recordings Act (aimed at controlling the availability of 'video-nasties') was mobilised by concern about their potentially disturbing influence on millions of impressionable young viewers. In spite of recent evidence which shows that television now contains *less* violence, the Broadcasting Standards Council is to monitor TV sex and violence. The evidence to support such short-term effects and direct influence is doubtful (see chapter four for a more detailed discussion of the evidence about media violence). Concentrating criticism, research and debate upon them ignores the wider influence that the media have in modern society. Once they are set in a broader social context, such 'short-term' effects appear less pressing.for two reasons.

First, the direct behavioural connection may be more apparent than real. There may be a deeper underlying social problem of which the media issue is merely an expression. For example, if the allegedly widespread problem of young people watching video-nasties at a friend's house, while Mum and Dad are out or downstairs minding their own business, is true, it points to two problems. Should impressionable youngsters have access to such material? But, more importantly, why are supposedly vulnerable young people 'unsupervised' for such long periods? Do we not need to create a society where parents are much more concerned about what their children are doing; where it is economically viable for one parent to choose to spend time with their children; where there are improved public-leisure facilities to compete with the dubious attractions of the 'box'? What appears initially to be a 'media issue', is a symptom of something much deeper.

Second, a wider social perspective allows us to look at media issues in more depth. Although some critics persist in claiming that the mass media are the harbingers of dramatic social change, most of the current research suggests rather the opposite – that the modern mass media merely reinforce and exacerbate the structures and divisions which already exist in society. The most persistent 'long-term' media effects may not come from violent movies or soft continental porn, but from adverts, soap operas, and news bulletins – from non-purposive, ideological communication. 'In portraying the predominantly accepted forms of power relationships in society, and legitimating means of reconciling conflicts of interest which are themselves part of those relationships, the media are an important contributor to the maintenance of societal consensus.'[22]

Many studies suggest that the media play a key role in creating a social consensus which legitimises the divisions of wealth, power and opportunity which currently exist in society. New technologies are incorporated into a social structure which functions to consolidate and exacerbate current inequalities. Christians who express concern for social justice will need to give much more attention to the way in which the modern mass media support, legitimise and enhance existing social injustice. They will need to confront the materialistic world view the media present. They will need to examine more closely the relationship between media content and the context in which it is produced. They will need to look at whose interests and needs the media serve. They will need to play their part in creating media structures which are more capable of being responsive and responsible to the *whole* community, rather than simply serving the financial or political aspirations of a few.

Chapter Four

Media Violence – Inciting or Insidious?

'To deny the power of television specifically to affect behaviour and to mould attitudes . . . is to deny the potency of communication itself.'

Mary Whitehouse[1]

'No case has been made where television (or the other media) could be legitimately regarded as a major contributory factor of any form of violent behaviour . . . At most they play a minor role.'

J.D. Halloran[2]

'Television has been identified, clearly and unambiguously as a cause of violence.'

W. Fore[3]

'It is interesting to note that when social scientists research the general subject of violence, they place Television low on the list of priorities.'

Wyatt Committee, BBC[4]

'The video containing combinations of violence and sex is a potential mental and moral health hazard of a kind we have not experienced before . . . our evidence establishes a clear case for censorship and stringent controls.'

G. Barlow & A. Hill[5]

'The evidence that TV causes aggression is not strong enough to justify restrictions in programming . . . It is

unlikely that war, murder, suicide, the battered child syndrome, other violent crimes and man's inhumanity to man stem to any marked degree from television viewing.'
                                        R.M. Kaplan & R.D. Singer[6]

On 18th August, 1987, in the small quiet market town of Hungerford, Michael Ryan, an apparently 'ordinary' young man suddenly went crazy. Armed with a Kalashnikov rifle, he stalked 'Rambo-style' through the town shooting family and strangers on sight. Within minutes some fourteen innocent men, women and children lay dead.

In the wake of such a seemingly inexplicable event many criticisms were levelled and questions asked. One question in particular sprang to prominence. Michael, a quiet, lonely young man, was known to be a strong TV and video fan. Did the violence he saw in films influence his tragic behaviour?

The BBC and IBA have long been sensitive to the controversy which surrounds screen violence. Early in 1987, the BBC published revised guidelines for producers, a guide for members of the public and commissioned fresh new 'independent' research.[7] In the wake of the tragedy at Hungerford, and out of respect for the feelings of those who had suffered as a result of the tragedy, the BBC and IBA axed a number of violent films and programmes due to be screened that evening and over the following days. Many saw it as a tacit admission of the link between television viewing and violent behaviour.

At the Conservative Party conference in October, 1987, Douglas Hurd, the then Home Secretary, announced not only new controls on the possession of firearms, but also the introduction of an independent watchdog committee to oversee TV sex and violence. His action won international acclaim.[8] At last someone was tackling the problem of excessive television violence. His announcement was widely welcomed, particularly by Christians.[9] Groups such as Mary Whitehouse's National Viewers' and Listeners' Association, the Order of Christian Unity, CARE (formerly the Nationwide Festival of Light) and the highly effective Parliamentary Video Group[10] had long been in the forefront of campaigns to 'clean-up' television and video. There was wide popular support for the 1984 Video Recordings Act, which extended the idea of censorship to cover (for the first time in Britain) material that people viewed in the privacy of their own homes. A BBC television survey showed that sixty-three per cent of viewers felt that violence on television led directly to an increase in violence in society.

Mary Whitehouse articulates popular, received wisdom, which suggests that for all the benefits TV can bring to society, its rich diet of violent images must have a direct bearing on increasing levels of social violence. There are two suggested areas of concern. First, that watching violent images directly affects behaviour. Viewers may be stimulated or aroused to perform similar acts of violence in real life. Second, that the prevalence of violent images will gradually have a detrimental effect upon viewers' attitudes and opinions. People will become de-sensitised and society more uncaring.

Television and Behaviour

Popular, received wisdom is invariably attractive and simple. However, it does not always correspond to reality. Closer scrutiny of evidence which seems to support the popular view that television contributes to violent behaviour (readily endorsed by many Christians) is based on a simplistic and often misleading understanding of the evidence. What is more disturbing, its constant repetition or refutation diverts attention from what are far more important relationships between violence and the media; and much more pertinent (and reliably documented) causes of violence in society. Society is straining at a gnat – it has yet to swallow the camel! Some media campaigners were more than a little taken aback when the Broadcasting Standards Council, the government's media watchdog, suggested that research evidence was not as conclusive as critics supposed.

On the face of it a direct link between screen violence and individual behaviour seems self-evident. TV is widely believed to be 'the most powerful medium to affect the thinking and behaviour of people'.[11] The advertisers who spend millions a year on television would certainly agree. They don't do so without good reason. If advertisements are so effective in persuading us to buy their products, isn't it also likely that the repeated portrayal of violent behaviour is just as influential? The seemingly obvious parallel is not only easy to grasp and explain but has provided the starting point for much research. However, the conclusions which emerge are by no means as clear cut as they are often made to appear. For example, one of the most quoted and extensive research programmes – the US Surgeon General's report – seems to be less often read than cited. It is often asserted that '700 international studies *prove* the link between television and violence'. In fact after examining all that evidence, the Surgeon General's Committee came to the rather weak conclusion that 'TV *may* lead to increased aggressive behavior in certain subgroups of children who *may* constitute a small portion or a substantial portion of young television viewers'.[12] And even that guarded statement is based upon an interpretation of the data which is open to question.[13]

The firmest-looking evidence for a direct link between violent behaviour and screen violence comes from experiments conducted in a laboratory. Carefully selected and controlled groups of people are shown a violent film clip and their behaviour, attitudes or willingness to act aggressively are subsequently measured or observed. This is compared either with a control group (who either didn't watch a film, or watched something 'soothing') or a measurement of aggression obtained previously. This model has formed the basis of countless studies, most of which have found evidence of a strong relationship between the violent material watched and a subject's subsequent behaviour. For some such evidence is conclusive[14] – but closer inspection of the way such convincing results are obtained suggests that they are of limited value. How far they can be applied to television in the real world is in serious doubt.

First, the sort of film clips involved often bear little relation to what people actually watch on TV. Even those that use broadcast material, use edited highlights, and effectively de-contextualise the image, altering the way people interpret and respond to what they see. Many studies use special films which are even more remote from typical TV fare. One famous experiment showed children a film of an adult attacking an inflatable doll! Second, the sort of aggressive behaviour they measure is quite unlike the 'real-life' incidents of rape, sexual assault, hooliganism, mugging and other inter-personal violence about which most people are concerned. In the famous 'doll' experiments, young children were shown the film and later encouraged to play with an identical doll. In another, students were encouraged by the experimenter to minister fake electric shocks to an unseen and unresisting member of the experimental team.

Third, the whole experimental context makes even this 'violent' behaviour unreal. The experimental environment is designed to ensure an *absence* of any social sanctions against aggression. Subjects are rather encouraged to be as aggressive as they like; there are no penalties, no re-criminations and no unpleasant personal consequences. In real life, however, people are deterred from aggression by a number of factors – fear of personal injury, resistance and retaliation on the part of their victim, the intervention of by-standers, a realisation of the consequences. In a laboratory experiment, subjects are encouraged to 'suspend' the values and judgments by which they normally live and which they bring to bear when they watch and respond to television. The results of these laboratory experiments may well tell us something about how people can be made to behave in certain ways, or how young children can be made to acquire novel aggressive responses. But they do not tell us much about the relationship between television and violence outside the laboratory in the real world. In fact, they raise more questions than they answer. Their results may be dramatic and easy to grasp but they have little application and validity beyond the laboratory walls.

Social scientists have shown a greater awareness of these limitations[15] than the campaigners who eagerly seize their results to confirm firmly-held opinions. But even if these limitations are not fully grasped, laboratory results are by no means as one way as they are often portrayed. Other experiments have shown just as convincingly that screen violence can have the *opposite* effect and may actually inhibit violent behaviour in some people, particularly when it is presented in a 'fantastic' or dramatic context. A much-quoted study of the viewing habits of London youngsters confirmed this. Those who watched the greatest amount of violent programmes were least likely to be involved in real-life violence.[16]

There have been attempts to get round these experimental limitations and discover the connection between TV viewing and aggression in everyday situations, but the difficulty of isolating television influence from other 'environmental' factors (peer-group pressure, upbringing etc) means they have not fared so well. Two of the most detailed studies[17] came to diametrically opposite conclusions about television's contribution, and their methodology and approach have attracted serious criticism from other researchers.[18] A study of video-nasties which purported to show that forty-five per cent of children had seen a video-nasty was eagerly seized upon by supporters of the 1984 Video Recordings Act.[19] However, because it failed adequately to test the validity and reliability of its data and employed great elasticity in its definition of a video-nasty (including a film subsequently shown on prime-time television!), it actually revealed little beyond the predispositions of its sponsors and their avowed need to provide data to whip up support for the Act.

Stories and anecdotes of TV's supposed 'triggering' effect simply add to the confusion. First, they can obscure a much more pertinent reason for individual aberrant behaviour (Ryan may have watched TV and video films, but he seems to have been a withdrawn, lonely figure, a fanatical collector of weapons and member of the local gun club). Second, they merely reinforce a simple 'cause/effect' model for understanding violence.

Studies in the fields of social psychology and criminology have focused on much broader issues and looked at wider attitudes and behaviour of young people – not just their use of the media. They suggest that we need a much more dynamic model of aggressive behaviour which takes adequate account of personality type, family upbringing, and social influences. Like all viewers, violent individuals are likely to be attracted to media images which confirm their world view. 'They won't see anything on the telly they haven't seen or haven't heard about where they live . . . Even in their own homes in many cases,' commented one inner-city police officer.[20] Rather than *cause* their aggressive behaviour, the media may simply *confirm* their experience of a world in which violence and aggression are an appropriate response.

A more fundamental flaw in the 'common-sense' argument that links screen violence to individual behaviour is a conceptual one. The seemingly obvious parallel between advertising and violent television may be more attractive than appropriate. Advertising doesn't seek to make us change our whole behaviour, and act against cultural mores and values. On the contrary, it often encapsulates, enshrines and reinforces many of those values and uses them to persuade viewers to spend their disposable income in a particular way. When they attempt more, they are ineffective (see chapter five). A more appropriate model for the way violent screen images are received is a health or political campaign which attempts to use the media to persuade people to change their minds, behave in radically different ways and go against prevailing attitudes. However, studies have repeatedly found that the mass media (and television in particular) are not as effective as had been supposed. Television's apparent power to change deeply held opinions is extremely limited. It is at its most effective reinforcing personal contact and persuasion. It best provides additional reassurance for those who have already been so persuaded.[21]

Violence in films and television may be distasteful to some viewers. They may wish to limit their own (or their children's) exposure to it. It is often gratuitous and sprinkled liberally into mediocre products to make them more appealing to advertisers and audiences. And it is often most disturbing in TV news reports (although most news editors maintain that their most violent footage ends up on the cutting-room floor, rather than our TV screens). But violence is a part of life. If the media are to bear any semblance to real life they will inevitably contain scenes of violence. The power of television news depends on its ability to shock us out of our complacency and confront us with the stark reality of the world that we've created.

The power of television fiction depends on its ability to engage our imagination in its conflict and drama. Bettelheim suggests that fantasy violence is an essential part of a child's healthy development. 'There is plenty of violence and crime in Old Testament stories, as well as in fairy tales. There is a lot of cruelty, enmity within the family, homicide, and even patricide and incest in Greek drama, as there is in Shakespeare's plays. This suggests that people have always needed a fare of violent fantasies as an integral part of popular entertainment . . . Children need as much of that relief as adults do – perhaps more – and they always will.'[22] The reality of God's love is depicted in a violent and gruesome image, that of an innocent, lonely man being slowly tortured to death on a cross.

An image draws its meaning, its power and its social acceptability as much from its context as its content. Debates about the limits of acceptability of violent media images are largely aesthetic and artistic debates – as much a debate about the meaning and function of the portrayal as the act itself. 'One man's media meat, is another man's media poison.' Those who advocate stricter social controls have spawned a surfeit of research to support the popular belief in the corruptible influence of the media. Closer scrutiny of the evidence upon which popular wisdom is based suggests that the apparently obvious link between individual behaviour and screen violence is in fact an illusion.[23] Perpetuating it simply ensures that other much more tenable and disturbing television influences are ignored.

Television and Attitudes

Whilst research into television's influence on violent behaviour has been marked by controversy, inappropriate methodology and sweeping generalisations, the study of the way TV influences our attitudes to violence has fared somewhat better. Television's very popularity and widely regarded 'trustworthiness' may have given it a highly significant social influence, one which many commentators find quite disturbing. Rather than simply giving a viewer a picture of the world outside the sitting room, the media's preoccupation with violent events gives a false impression of social reality. This impression may be highly influential in our understanding of and reactions to the violence of modern society.

We shall look in greater detail at the news media in chapter six, but since they form the basis for much of our understanding of the wider world[24] and since they have been identified by viewers as a major source of violent imagery[25] we also need to assess their place in any relationship which may exist between screen and real-life violence. In seeking to interpret and explain raw events, the news media often look for familiar frameworks or 'angles'. Initial reporting then becomes the paradigm and colours the way subsequent events are portrayed. Certain features dominate, others are ignored. Links and parallels are made between different and perhaps unrelated events. The stereotyping and misrepresentation which are inherent in this process are not only influential in forming public awareness, but also influences the expectations of politicians and the police and affects their reactions and responses to the event. Apart from an inevitable concentration on dramatic events rather than important issues, this feature of news production has two noticeable consequences.

First, it selects violent incidents as especially 'news-worthy'.[26] Other events are then tarnished with the same violent brush. When English football supporters followed their team to Sweden in 1989, British newspapers expected trouble. Sure enough, the media were awash with stories of fans on the rampage, trouble and arrests. Their behaviour was condemned at Question Time in the Commons. The voices of Swedish policemen protesting that the fans had been, by and large, peaceful, that they had made few arrests, and that trouble had stemmed from Swedish fans were drowned in the tabloid scramble for copy and pictures.

A landmark study of the notorious 'Grosvenor Square' student demonstration of 1968 compared media images with what actually happened. It found that images of violence dominated television and press coverage. In the wake of student riots in Paris, press speculation about a possible violent confrontation set the context for media coverage. Considering the large numbers present, there was in fact very little violence; the demonstration was a largely peaceful affair. However, because the few violent incidents which did occur offered dramatic pictures and fitted the 'frame' already set by the media, violent incidents dominated media coverage and eventually coloured people's reactions to the whole event. In subsequent discussion and reflection, the reasons for the demonstration were all but lost. The study warned: 'The way the media dealt with the situation led to labelling, to the unjustifiable association of certain groups with violent behaviour . . . to acceptance of violence as . . . a legitimate way of dealing with problems or as a necessary form of retaliation . . . This violence "framework" may effectively remove political demonstration from the range of political dissent.'[27] They were prophetic words. In the twenty years since 'Grosvenor Square', media images have confirmed for most people that 'political demonstration' is a synonym for 'violence'. By similarly highlighting violent incidents, media coverage of the miners' strike in 1985, the 'peace convoy' in 1986 and the Wapping printers' dispute etc have played their part in mobilising support for the public order and anti-trade union legislation. The state is now in a position to effectively veto any demonstration or mass public expression of political dissent.

Second, the news production process also sets limits upon the ways in which the public understand and interpret an event. News media do not present impartial images of the world but, through the comments and suggestions they offer, try to help us understand the significance of what is going on. Because they are heavily dependent upon the state as a source of news, these 'comments' and 'suggestions' almost invariably reflect an official 'government' perspective. Indeed, the state is not beyond applying a bit of pressure to try to make sure that their perspective is the only one heard. Government and police action against the BBC over the *Real Lives* and *Zircon* documentaries, and their attempts to suppress *Death on the Rock* show how determined they can be. Their views are most readily available, most authoritative, most eager to be heard.

Studies over a whole range of issues from crime to Church affairs, from social policy to education, have demonstrated that although the state's definition of the issues, problems and solutions is not the only one to be aired on the media, it invariably predominates. Programmes such as *Question Time, Kilroy, Any Questions?* and ever-more popular radio phone-ins attempt a balanced perspective. But they cannot compete with the volume of news and current affairs programmes which are broadcast at peak viewing and listening times. The Prime Minister and cabinet even dominate news images of parliament. As Lord Scarman's enquiry into civil disorder in Britain reported, the circumstances in which social violence is set are complicated and confused. There is a need to listen to and understand the problems of those who are affected and involved. The media's dependence upon power élites (the police and government spokespeople) as a prime source of newsworthy comments ensures that they set the tone for how such behaviour is to be understood and what response is necessary and appropriate. Debate (if any) usually revolves around their limited definitions.

The way violence is portrayed in the media exerts a powerful influence on people's perception of the world and their response to it. The media's mapping of problematic and violent events within the conventional understanding of society is crucial in two ways. The media not only define for the majority of the population *what* significant events are taking place, but also offer powerful interpretations of *how* to understand those events. Violence is defined; the threat it poses to society is clearly spelled out. And the way in which the media set it out means that they effectively canvass support for an 'appropriate' response to that threat.

A study of the way television and the press covered mugging in the early 'seventies set this process of media influence in a much broader perspective. It argued that the agenda that the media set for public debate about such controversial issues – or 'moral panics' – has a cumulative effect. The various separate violent incidents and disorders, rather than being understood and explained in their own contexts, are grouped together as part of a wider picture of society. (The preacher who denounces the sin of the world by reference to last night's television news, performs a similar function.) Every act which can be labelled as 'violent' becomes an index of widespread social anarchy and disorder. Any form of protest labelled in this way becomes a law and order issue. The labelling of 'deviant' behaviour and legitimation of an increasingly coercive official response 'becomes a means by which a silent majority is won over to the support of increasingly coercive measures on the part of the state, and lends its legitimacy to a more than usual exercise of control'.[28]

The thesis is provocative and, whilst not without its critics, finds unlikely support in studies which have looked at the influence of fictional television violence. These suggest that the manner in which violence is portrayed is also highly significant. First, viewers are presented with a context in which violence is considered a justifiable or appropriate response. A comparison between Russian and American television shows that, whilst in the USSR televised violence is generally presented in historical and collective contexts, in the USA (and consequently in much of the western media!) the emphasis is on inter-personal aggression set in the context of personal success, achievement and the maintenance of private property. In both systems, media violence reinforces an existing social order – together with their respective inequalities and injustices.[29]

Second, violence is widely used in the western media to create excitement and attract and keep an audience. This creates a misleading impression about the incidence of violence in real life. A long-term American study has compared the different attitudes of those who watch a lot of television with those who watch little. It found that television had an 'homogenising' effect, that it helped to create a uniform view of the world and that the high incidence of screen violence was particularly significant. It concludes, disturbingly, that 'on the whole, the most general and prevalent association with television viewing is a heightened sense of living in a "mean world" of violence and danger.'[30] It is often those who are most dependent upon the media as a prime source of contact with the world who are made to feel most insecure, rather than those who are at greatest risk. Whilst crime figures show that young people (particularly women and blacks) are most likely to be victims of aggression, it is the elderly who are made to feel most insecure – particularly since the rarer incidents of violent attacks are given such sensational coverage by the media.

Getting to see one elderly housebound member of my church in a quiet Norfolk market town was like trying to break into the Bank of England! She recounted in great detail the violent stories she had heard or read about in the media. Anxiety, out of all proportion to any real risk, had displaced sensible precaution. She was isolated and imprisoned by her own debilitating fear – too scared even to pop round the corner to collect her pension. Such fear exacts a high cost from the society which engenders it. 'This unequal and corrosive sense of insecurity and mistrust invites not only aggression but also exploitation and repression. Fearful people are more dependent, more easily manipulated and controlled, more susceptible to deceptively simple, strong, tough measures and hard-line postures – both political and religious. They may accept and even welcome repression if it promises to relieve their insecurities. That is the deepest problem of violence-laden television.'[31]

Paradoxically, the increased social attention on law-enforcement measures as a result of the perceived increase in violence may well divert support (and ultimately scarce resources) from social programmes such as improved housing, day-care centres etc which would actually *prevent* crime. As noted above, even the style of policing that society demands to meet this social 'threat' may itself be counter-productive. In recent years, serious urban disturbances in Britain have usually been triggered by police use of controversial 'stop/search' powers.

Deeper Values

Today's mass media, newspapers, magazines, advertisement hoardings and especially television may, however, make a much more fundamental contribution to violence in our society that the obsession with screen violence makes us overlook. In a consumer society material prosperity is equated with happiness; possessions with fulfilment; consumption with participation. These underlying values dominate the media. Through advertising, games shows, soap operas about rich élites, the oft-repeated myth of an open society where riches await anyone who works for them and the cult of media 'stars' who spend thousands on a West-End birthday or wedding bash dominate the popular press and present us with an abundance of examples to reinforce the message. However, increasing numbers of viewers are denied that opportunity to participate. The 1969 US National Commission on the Causes and Prevention of Violence was unable to find a direct behavioural link with the media. It suggested instead that social violence is located in a context of frustrated expectations, social deprivation, rapid social change (giving rise to unattainable expectations) and a sharp relative decline in socio-economic or political conditions, coupled with a feeling of alienation from political processes – the very conditions that currently exist in many of Britain's cities (as 'Faith in the City' graphically described[32]). Whilst television does not directly cause these inner-city problems, there is a sharp contrast between the screen world and viewers' expectations. The conspicuous portrayal of opulent consumption in the face of seemingly intractable social disadvantage and ever-deepening social divisions is likely to play its part in creating feelings of injustice and frustration – factors which the American Commission found to be a significant root cause of violence.

Senior police officers working in one of Liverpool's most deprived areas felt that this was probably television's greatest contribution to crime.

> If they've got nothing else in the home, they'll always have a telly . . . almost invariably tuned to a commercial network. This means that for upwards of ten minutes in every hour the viewer is subjected to advertising material which has the sole aim of making everyone feel a 'have-not', let alone those least able legitimately to change their quality of life on impulse. In wretched circumstances, given the subliminal effect of so much advertising and the cumulative effect of yearning built up over the years, it can't take much to see a shop window as a sort of large TV screen with one vital difference: it can be broken and plundered.[33]

This, however, is not the sort of relationship which people usually have in mind when they speculate or pontificate about the link between media and violence.[34]

A direct and simple 'cause and effect' model between screen violence and violence in society does not stand up to scrutiny. It stands apart from research in other disciplines which suggests a much more complex web of influences of violent behaviour. It relies on an obsolete model of television influence and stands outside more recent developments in our understanding of the way the media influence and affect society. These suggest that the constant repetition of the 'cause and effect' model has three disturbing effects.

First, it has diverted public attention from the deeper underlying social issues such as poverty, inadequate housing, unemployment and apparent political alienation – factors which lie at the root of many modern expressions of violence.

Second, it has effectively obscured from public view a much more subtle and indirect consequence of media violence: the justification of the current social order, the vindication of existing inequalities, the labelling of liminal groups as deviant and the legitimation of repressive state violence as a justifiable, inevitable and necessary response to threat. It is much easier to identify and criticise the media in foreign countries than it is in our own, particularly when we are largely unable to compare and correct our own coverage with overseas images of ourselves.

Third, it has ignored any analysis of a wider relationship between other media content, media values, and their more subtle effect on behaviour, attitudes and social violence.

Chapter Five

It's the real thing . . . Advertising and the Media

'The television commercial is the most peculiar and persuasive form of communication to issue from the electric
plug.'

N. Postman[1]

' . . . commercials . . . not only serve to inform the public
but also amuse and entertain . . . '

IBA Yearbook[2]

' . . . advertising is produced with primarily pecuniary ends
in mind; it is created explicitly to enhance the financial
status of the patron.'

Quentin J. Schultze[3]

' . . . the display advertisements in the press, the jingles on
radio, the TV commercials, the posters in our streets and
the flickering lights in our city squares . . . are the most
obvious part of our communication environment.'

Media Development[4]

Advertisements have become 'the single most voluminous
form of public communication in our society.'[5] The proportion of space which they occupy in British newspapers
has been growing over the years so that they now account
for about half the content of a typical Sunday newspaper.[6]
They also form about ten per cent of the total output of
commercial television and radio. One and a half of the

twenty-six hours of television an average viewer watches in a week will be advertisements. In fact commercial radio and television devote nearly as much time to advertising as they do to news or current affairs, and considerably more than to feature films or sport![7] All this makes advertising BIG business. Global spending on advertising is currently running at over $500,000,000 per day.[8] In Britain advertising accounts for approximately two per cent of all consumer spending.[9] It is beginning to account for an increasing level of government expenditure, too. In 1989, the government was Britain's biggest advertiser, spending nearly £75 million on advertising its policies, schemes and privatisation plans. In 1985, over £3,130 million was spent in Britain on advertisements on television, the press and radio, with TV taking the lion's share. The sale of viewers' attention and time generated the commercial TV companies a revenue of £1,156 million, dwarfing the income the BBC received from the sale of TV licences by £250 million. Most Christians probably contributed more to advertisements than they did to the Church!

The Influence of Advertising

In view of their prevalence and huge financial clout, any attempt to understand the media needs to take a closer look at the influence of advertising in two areas.

First, the effect that advertisements have on society – the way that their messages influence the viewers, readers and listeners who make up their 'consumers'. This has been the traditional and obvious concern of the advertisers themselves. For them effects are synonymous with the effectiveness of their campaigns. Others point out, however, that advertisements frequently promote 'a whole way of life'. Some have seen them as harmful to traditional social mores and suggest that issues such as parental authority, social morality and the legitimation of particular 'lifestyles' are at stake.

But advertising also has a second, much more indirect, level of influence. Advertisers' interests have influenced the development, structure, content and diversity of the media system itself. Whilst advertisers in Britain are swift to deny any direct overt attempt to influence media content, research suggests that with such large sums at stake, their influence is subtle and profound.

1. Advertising and society

Advertisers – and the media that depend upon them (commercial television and radio, the press, magazines, journals etc) – argue that advertisements are basically benign. The IBA, in an echo of Reithian paternalism, see their function as informing and entertaining viewers by showing them a range of goods and services. Some have gone further and argue that advertisements make a positive contribution to the wellbeing of society. Galbraith, for example, argues that the primary function of advertising is to create desires which previously did not exist. Before Amstrad came along, how many ministers and writers of Christian books *knew* that they needed a word processor? When they invented the Walkman, Sony did not so much meet an expressed human need for perpetual, personal music as manufacture one! By encouraging the sale of mass-produced goods, advertising, it is argued, stimulates production and creates employment and prosperity. By giving people a desire for goods and services they would not otherwise have dreamt of, they encourage people to work harder, and have played their part in creating a prosperous society. Those who *produce* the goods are also the ones who consume them. Further, the encouragement of *mass* consumption through the *mass* media ensures a rapid turnover of consumable items (soap powder, toothpaste, manufactured food products etc). Less capital is tied up in the distribution system and can be released for investment, production and, ultimately, further consumption.

Mass advertising has become an essential ingredient of

the economics of *mass* production. It has helped to create the very wealth it so opulently displays. Anyway, advertisers argue, advertisements cannot possibly *harm* anyone. They can't *force* people to go out and buy their products and services. People are perfectly free to ignore them. The fact that so many well-thought-out campaigns actually fail is evidence enough that they don't 'brainwash' people. In spite of good copy and excellent exposure, Guinness's attempt in the 'seventies to make their product more appealing to women proved an expensive flop![10]

The first task of constructive criticism and any attempt to apprehend reality is to be cautious about accepting the given parameters of a debate – particularly when those who give them have such a vested interest. Whilst advertisers may primarily be interested in the 'effectiveness' of a campaign, that does not mean that advertisements have no other effects. Like all communication, advertisements need to be seen in a much broader context. They are just as likely to have long-term and diffuse effects. There is mounting evidence that advertisements help to define social reality. They project goals and values consistent with and conducive to a consumer economy and help to socialise us into thinking that we can 'buy' a way of life in the same way that we buy goods.[11] To get a true picture of advertising influence, we need to look at broad, long-term, social effects – not just last month's sales figures.

Second, the IBA claim that advertisements carry consumer 'information' is grossly misleading. Whilst it is true that *some* advertisements offer information about products (notably those that appear in 'trade' journals or make up the classified columns of newspapers) these are addressed to 'users' who actively seek information about products, relative merit, availability etc, rather than 'consumers'. The bulk of advertising (particularly the sort of advertising with which the IBA is concerned) is rather directed at 'consumers'. It is made up of adverts for 'consumables' – detergents, washing-up liquid, pet food, tea, coffee, alcohol and the like. Adverts for these products usually contain very little 'information', and are directed to maintaining 'brand loyalty'. In 1985, £337,736,000 was spent by just four 'holding' companies (Unilever, Mars GB, Imperial Group and Procter & Gamble), advertising everyday commodities in an attempt to make us more aware of their own particular brand – trying to make us think about Comfort rather than fabric softener, Nescafé rather than coffee, Whiskas rather than cat food. The latest Carling Black Label advert may well turn out to be the most entertaining part of an evening's viewing – but it hardly justifies being called 'informative'.

While advertisements for consumer products still provide the bulk of TV advertising revenue, the biggest single consumer of viewers' time and attention is now the government. Adverts about drug misuse, job clubs, employment training, poll-tax rebates and family credit have no proven success at influencing behaviour – they merely perpetuate the illusion that the government is doing something. 'Cheaper to advertise than tackle the problem,' comments one critic.

Adverts which suggest that there will be a rush of customers for the latest private sale of publicly owned essential services (gas, water, electricity) are as much an attempt to persuade viewers of a particular policy as they are to inform them about the sale.

Third, the limited range of products which appear in advertisements and the fact that they are largely 'consumer' items offers merely an *illusion* of choice – simply more of the same kind of thing. Gillian Dyer argues that 'our real freedom of choice is by and large sacrificed to the flow of chocolate, shampoos, breakfast cereals and dog foods which gushes out of the factories . . . Producers and consumers are more often than not trapped in the illusion that more and more consumer goods automatically guarantees choice and freedom.'[12] In choosing between different brands from the barrage of consumable and durable goods on offer we are never presented with the choice of whether we want yet more. The consumer ideal not only ignores social needs – it actively denies them.

As personal expenditure becomes exalted, corporate

expenditure (on hospitals, education, social services, etc) becomes despised. The really important decision to invest valuable resources in the creation of a new product rather than a youth club, say, has already been made. The creation of an 'all over body spray' was neither a creative impulse nor a response to consumer demand, but a carefully researched, corporate decision about the best way to break into a market which was already overcrowded with traditional scent and deodorant products.[13]

Fourth, advertisements set out to imbue goods and artifacts with cultural significance and status. They offer us an image and try to associate a 'lifestyle' with a particular product. Thus cheap canvas work wear become 'designer jeans'; a car becomes a status and sexual symbol, the main character in a sixty-second mini-drama of sexual intrigue and deception; frozen food – the mark of a liberated lifestyle. Material things that we 'need' come to represent and offer fulfilment for non-material desires and aspirations. Diamonds become the symbol of eternal love; perfume – of acceptance and desirability; liquid detergent – a successful home manager; an insurance policy – wisdom and security.

Advertisements do not try to sell us things – they sell us ourselves and offer us an image of what we would like to become. They are not about the character of products, they are about the character of consumers. Advertising attaches feelings, moods or attributes to tangible objects and links possibly *un*attainable things with those that *are* attainable. They assure us that the former are within reach.[14]

If you want to be a *perfect* mum – then your washing needs to be white and odour-free. If you want to be an ideal lover – splash on brand X. In trading on our insecurities and aspirations, advertisements offer powerful images of what the perfect mum and ideal lover *should* be like. 'What is missing . . . are all those statistical evils that social science has so carefully enumerated: rising promiscuity, divorce, adolescent sexuality, the prevalence of drugs . . . the universal experience of crime . . . hunger, want, unemployment.'[15] The media images that advertisements project convey a picture of a world 'flourishing' in spite of its underlying problems.

Although viewers do not passively absorb these images as a 'true' picture of the world (see pages 26ff.), their juxtaposition with other media images of conflict and deprivation in news and current affairs programmes creates a false illusion of security. They enhance our desire to participate in the respite and illusory comfort that they offer.

Some critics (e.g. Galbraith, Dyer, Berman, Williams) have suggested that advertising confuses *desires* with *needs*, that the common human psychological and spiritual needs to feel secure, to be loved and accepted, are exploited by advertisements. Their products are presented as the key to a pleasant and worthwhile personal life. They reiterate and perpetuate the cultural myth 'that the purchase of products will lead the buyer to health, success, beauty and social respect'.[16] Ironically, advertising also highlights the inconsistencies inherent in this consumptive illusion. If material goods were *really* able to satisfy our deepest needs, then cultural signification would be unnecessary.

> Beer would be enough for us, without the additional promise that in drinking it we show ourselves to be manly, young in heart, or neighbourly. A washing machine would be a useful machine to wash clothes, rather than an indication that we are forward-looking or an object of envy to our neighbours. But if these associations sell beer and washing machines, as some of the evidence suggests, it is clear that we have a cultural pattern in which the objects are not enough but must be validated, if only in fantasy, by association with social and personal meanings which in a different cultural pattern might be more directly available.[17]

Modern advertisements not only highlight the fallacy of consumerism – the fact that material goods are unable to satisfy basic human needs – they also divert attention and efforts away from the ways in which those needs *could* be met.

The same is also true of social needs. Advertisements offer us *personal* solutions to what are really *social* problems. Lead-free petrol will save the environment. Optrex will combat pollution; Flora and All-Bran – the effects of an unhealthy national diet; a telephone call – the disintegration of close family ties and the loneliness and neglect of the elderly; private health care – a crumbling national health service; personal-pension plans – inadequate social provision for retirement. 'The semiotics of "advertising and consumerism" in (the) media also construct our culture, creating commodity fetishes and false consciousness unimaginable even to Marx himself. In a bad mood? Go shopping. Want status? Upgrade your wardrobe, your car, your house, and if necessary, your mate.'[18]

2. *The effects of advertising images*

Once adverts are seen in these broader contexts, then their social 'effects', rather than their immediate persuasive effectiveness, become a much more pressing area of Christian and ethical concern.

First, advertisements address us as 'consumers'. We are encouraged by them to see ourselves as playing a limited (and limiting) role in the productive cycle. Some claim that this portrayal 'masks' our true economic role; most of us are also 'producers'. Others point out that it reinforces the idea that participation in society is effected principally through consumption. Advertisements transform human beings into consumers in two ways. Like pornography, advertising images often treat people (particularly women) as objects. A recent strand in feminist critiques of the way advertising has appropriated the female form has focused not only on explicit representation but also the way slogans like 'underneath they're all loveable' (for Loveable bras) have reduced women to the status of objects. But the de-humanisation implicit in many advertisements is also reinforced by the very concept of mass advertising. Adverts are tuned to a *mass* market – not individuals. They are aimed at a 'target' audience – not human beings. They are designed to 'overcome forces of sales resistance', not to enable rational people to make meaningful decisions about how they wish to live their lives.

All this stands in sharp contrast to a Biblical concept of humanity which sees people using their moral and intellectual capabilities as governors of God's world.[19] It is much closer to the idea that wherever people are overpowered by the things which they themselves are meant to overpower, inhumanity is born.[20]

Second, the central place that advertisements have in our media system carries its own powerful message. They are not so much inducements to buy goods, as statements about *why* goods are produced, whom they benefit and how they fit into our lives.[21] Their message is that private acquisition and competitiveness are primary goals in life. They present a social world of stability and order and inform us that CONSUMPTION is its basis. Kavanaugh spells out the devastating consequences of their tempting ideology. 'We *are* only insofar as we possess. We are *what* we possess. We are consequently possessed by our possessions, produced by our products. Remade in the image and likeness of our own handiwork, we are revealed as commodities. Idolatory exacts its full price from us. We are robbed of our very humanity.'[22]

Through their images, texts and very presence, advertisements communicate ideas about the things necessary for life. It is against this persuasive background that the modern Church proclaims its anachronistic message not to be anxious about tomorrow (Matt. 6:24-34) and calls people to repent and reject the 'commodity form'. It is not simply that the Churches' *style* of presentation is often at variance with communication today, rather the Gospel message itself is out of place. To suggest that all people – irrespective of status, wealth and purchasing power – are special to God and have meaning and value in and of themselves flies in the face of today's collective, social 'reality' and the prevailing ideology which is the stock in trade of the advertiser's world.

The once-dreaded Seven Deadly Sins have become the motivational deep structure of a culture of commercialism and consumption. Greed, lust, gluttony, envy, and all the once-presumed 'lower' urges have been reclaimed from Hieronymus Bosch and made all-gorgeous through the cleverness of Madison Avenue, Wall Street and their advertising. The classic Beatitudes – blessed are the meek, the humble, the peacemakers – have no place in this promotional culture of . . . media narcissism and consumption.[23]

Third, advertising not only necessarily reinforces the current social status quo in its exoneration of acquisitive competitiveness, it also offers simple solutions to life's eternal problems. Advertisements offer an artificial, stereotypical world in many respects superior to our own (how many of our kitchens ever look as tidy and modern as those on TV!). They offer us models and images and invite us to identify with them. They present not an outward-going but an inward-looking world, not a wide vista but a view which is narrow and constrained. They do not open up more possibilities but limit the perceptions of those which already exist.[24]

Whilst not all members of an audience receive meaning in the same way, it seems likely that the 'repetitive patterns of advertising' which so readily reinforce a prevailing social ethic have the cumulative effect of a dripping tap. They *encourage* their audience to conceive of themselves according to very limited categories. Thus even the modern 'liberated' woman who now populates our adverts still largely conforms to an idealised 'sexually available' type.[25]

Many of the most perceptive and trenchant criticisms of adverts have exposed their underlying ideologies – taking to task the images they produce and the effects that these are likely to have on people's aspirations, identities and self-image. As they promote a world of domestic private enjoyment, they hasten the privatisation of social life and the decay of the public sphere. If adverts are as motivationally successful as the agencies advocate and some critics warn, then they also have the capacity to raise unrealistic expectations and exacerbate social divisions. Not only do they successfully project the kind of life into which most of us are exhorted to 'buy', they also project it to those who have not the means to do so. One notable media scholar has suggested that this may be the *real* (though as yet largely undiscovered) link between the media and violence in society.[26] Even as we laugh at the Black Label advert, even as we dismiss the latest claims of a 'miracle detergent', or wonder what cats prefer Whiskas to, we are absorbing, participating in, and (by default) condoning a prevailing ideology which puts goods above people, individual choice above the 'common good', and papers over the divisions and tensions which exist in our society. Our stewardship and Christian giving may be directed to hastening God's kingdom on earth; but the advertisements we subsidise through our daily purchases make its establishment less likely, its inauguration more remote.

The claim that advertisements simply 'inform and entertain' and that they are 'beneficial' must be judged against their wider social significance. We must face the real question: who ultimately benefits from the advertising of consumer goods – society as a whole, or a few powerful commodity manufacturers and business corporations? As we examine the influence that advertising exercises over our whole media system, the question is brought into sharper focus.

'Advertisers have never in practice sought to influence the content of programmes or the editorial independence of programme makers.'

B. Henry[27]

'From the beginning of the mass-publicity system advertisers have required the media they use to provide a sympathetic context for the reception of their messages.'

G. Murdock[28]

'Advertising does have a direct effect on editorial environment.

The more we spent on advertising the more editorial copy
ran and the more it supported us.'

T. Wilson[29]

Indirect Influences of Advertising

Many critics have argued that the very presence of adverts in media which are supposed to impart neutral and
'independent' information poses a potential conflict of interests. Whilst advertisers acknowledge their preference
for a 'sympathetic context'[30] they stress that this does not
extend to attempts to influence content. Senior IBA officials
reject the notion of any direct influence,[31] but as the Royal
Commission on the Press pointed out, it would hardly be in
an advertiser's or media organisation's interests to publicise
such incidents if they did occur.[32]

Because of the way TV and radio time is sold, commercial broadcasters are in a very strong position to resist
any editorial pressure from advertisers. (Their position is
further strengthened when they hold a monopoly of TV and
radio advertising – as they did before the 1990 Broadcasting Act. Advertisers who wished to appear on television
were unable to take their custom elsewhere!) Newspapers,
however, have shown themselves much more susceptible
to direct advertising influence. Hird claims that the *Sunday
Times* revised its policy about campaigning against cigarette
advertising in response to W.D. & H.O. Wills's decision
to withdraw half a million pounds of booked advertising.[33]
Tony Wilson suggests that the London evening papers,
originally hostile to the GLC and strongly in favour of its
abolition, changed their editorial position partly to attract
their share of its advertising budget.[34]

Although by their very nature examples of direct media influence are sketchy and, on the whole, appear less
significant and secure than critics have argued, there are
other much more significant, though subtle, influences that
advertisements can bring to bear.

1. The press

Newspapers are totally dependent upon the amount (and type) of advertising that they can attract (between forty and seventy-five per cent of the cost of production is met from advertising revenue). When it collapsed in 1964, the *Daily Herald* had more than twice as many readers as *The Times, Financial Times* and *Guardian* put together, but it failed to attract sufficient advertising revenue to make it viable.[35] The effect of the influence that advertisers can bring to bear on newspaper content can be seen most clearly in the rapid growth of 'editorial features' that relate directly to the advertising material that surround them – those articles about holidays, gardening, motoring and, especially, personal finance. A recent survey found that up to one third of all editorial matter in 'quality' papers is linked to advertisements in this way.[36] Specialist journalists working in these areas have developed a much more 'uncritical' style of journalism.[37] Motor manufacturers who fly journalists and cars to exotic locations to launch their latest models certainly get their money's worth!

The whole pattern of the 'quality' press, the range of issues that they address and the significance they attach to them has been shaped by their need to attract advertisers who wish to reach a significant, small number of high-spending readers. In their desire to attract lucrative 'personal-investment' advertising, for example, ninety per cent of the financial and business sections in the national press are dedicated to providing tips, hints and commentary to service the 'personal investor'. Apart from belying the traditional notion of impartial investigative journalism (to which many readers still cling) this also creates a distorted impression of the way the economy works and grossly exaggerates the insignificant role that the small private investor has in the British economy. By contrast, industrial investment, which is actually central to the level of production, inflation and employment in Britain, receives little, if any, attention.[38] This distorted economic view – achieved without covert advertising pressure, no conspiracy and no suppression of facts – has seeped deep into public consciousness and has reinforced a political economic agenda concentrating on the individual investor.

At the other end of the market, popular newspapers have responded to a different marketing imperative. Their news coverage reflects advertisers' needs to reach the higher spending groups of the general population.[39] Research has consistently shown that news about politics and public affairs has little appeal to women and young people (the 'higher spenders') whilst human interest and entertainment features have considerable appeal across all readers. News and current affairs coverage has therefore been severely cut back. The consequent increase in entertainment and human interest coverage provides 'a powerful confirmation of the world view that advertising promotes . . . Both concentrate on the spheres of leisure and consumption, both celebrate the pleasures of possession and both represent social divisions as differences of life style rather than life chances, the products of individual choices rather than structured inequalities'.[40]

2. Television

Supported by tighter regulation, commercial television was structurally better equipped to resist direct advertising intervention. However, the style and ethos of many popular entertainment programmes mirror the consumerist advertising world which underpins them. The winner of consumer games shows are the 'everyday heroes' of consumerism whose delight in winning a holiday, a CD player or video recorder is powerful visual confirmation of the delight and satisfaction that possession conveys. The desire of advertisers to reach the largest mass audience possible also means that programmes are designed to appeal to the widest cross-section of the audience. The Pilkington report on advertising and broadcasting made it clear that the commercial objectives of 'independent' television and radio companies rendered 'quality' and 'quantity' mutually exclusive and irreconcilable objectives.[41] Ironically, the BBC, too, has recently become subject to the same pressures. In the face of outright political hostility and in order to justify its claim for continued public funding it has been forced to compete for greater market share. A nightly diet of soap, Wogan and games shows may push up the ratings but, as one critic put it, its output 'is rapidly becoming more bland, superficial and undemanding'.[42]

Some critics have also suggested that this commercial development may also have limited television's ability to deal with certain questions. Freed from the shackles of promoting a commodity ethic, television might well have devoted more space and time to giving consumer information in the same way that it provides reviews of cultural events and information (the theatre, horse racing or the stock exchange). The argument that news and entertainment media are merely giving the 'public what it wants' – and are subject to the 'sovereignty of the consumer' – are fallacies and ignore (or simplify) the effects of advertising influence on media content. The world view that advertisers promote inevitably transfers itself to the media in which they appear, and through their large financial 'subsidy' they effectively determine the range of media which are available to the public.

3. Media choice

Advertisers argue that consumer preference is the real determinant in media availability. The Institute of Practitioners of Advertising rightly claims that the advertising subsidy has brought more newspapers and magazines to the public[43] – but that is only half the story. Advertisers are not equally interested in reaching all people. Some people have more disposable income or greater power over corporate spending than others. Advertisers are either interested in reaching a mass audience or affluent minorities. They pay scant attention to groups with little purchasing power: the poor, the elderly or disadvantaged.[44]

Advertising is aimed at elderly people with disposable investment income and not at the vast majority of elderly people in Britain who live at or near the poverty line. Multiplicity – in which a few 'high spending' groups are well catered for – is confused with diversity. This has led to a wealth of 'consumer' magazines, particularly for women and young people and a corresponding dearth of material covering issues such as politics, old age, poverty etc. People's range of information and entertainment choices is severely tied to their ability to consume. The greater their purchasing power – the more media choices they have. The rich and business executives are the only minority groups fully catered for.[45]

4. Sponsorship

Whilst patronage has long been associated with cultural and sporting events, sponsorship – where money is invested in return for publicity – is relatively new. Its recent introduction into television and rapid growth has been given added impetus by a Conservative administration which has encouraged private enterprise to take over the traditional public support for social and cultural amenities.[46] Clauses in the 1990 Broadcasting Act mean that TV sponsorship will continue to grow. News of winter gales (and their attendant power cuts) is provided courtesy of Power Gen!

Sponsorship of entertainment and arts offers companies two benefits. First, it is regarded as a PR exercise. Association with a 'quality' event or product allows the sponsor to bask in their reflected prestige. Not only does this allow them to demonstrate their concern for the 'quality of life' (especially important for companies with a particularly tarnished environmental image – such as tobacco and oil) but it also enables them to target events which attract an upmarket élite clientele (the London arts, opera and orchestras) enhancing their image with key City decision makers.

Second (and more important), it enables firms whose

products are traditionally banned from television advertising (e.g. cigarettes) to reach an audience of many millions – through the BBC as well as ITV. A recent survey suggested that schoolchildren's familiarity with certain cigarette brands was partly the result of television's extensive snooker coverage. Whilst legislators attempt to control the adverse effects of alcohol on crowd violence by banning its sale at soccer matches, team members are tightening the link between having a drink and watching a match by promoting brand names – on and off the pitch!

An even more recent development in advertising techniques is called 'product placement'. Film, television and radio producers are paid to ensure that a particular product (a brand of soft drink, lager, car, or toy, say) becomes an incidental (though noticeable feature) in a film or programme. The hero always drives the same car, flies with the same airline, or drinks the same drink. In the USA, this has meant that some children's television programmes have become little more than commercials for (expensive) children's toys and are now being made by the toy manufacturers and offered to TV stations at knock-down prices. Toy retailers are routinely advised by manufacturers when such series are due to be shown. Toys have even been developed that will interact with the television programmes. So-called 'independent' producers may well turn out to be less independent that they first appear.

Legal, Decent, Honest and Destructive

'The broadcast and print media have increasingly turned viewers and readers into a product to be delivered to the sponsors, so that the objective . . . has been changed from informing, enlightening and entertaining simply to reaching and holding the largest audience regardless of the damage done to other . . . objectives.'[47] The values of consumer advertising not only affect society through the images which they present and perpetuate, their underlying ideology permeates the whole media system – they affect the very quality and range of media which are available. As public broadcasting declines and new media systems develop to meet commercial demand rather than public interest, their values are likely to dominate the media still further. They may be legal, decent and honest. That doesn't stop them being insidious, divisive and socially malign.

Chapter Six

Tell it like it is . . . The News

'To a very large extent, broadcast news is a fragmentation of reality . . . '
P. Golding & P. Elliott[1]

'The recent research on news production and content concludes almost unanimously that there is a systematic distortion in the news representation of public reality.'
R.A. White[2]

'Newspapers are shoddy goods sold cheap and should be read accordingly.'
Harold Jackson[3]

'Television news gives a partial view of the world: it offers an open door to the powerful and a closed door to the rest of us.'
Glasgow University Media Group[4]

'In the midst of mass society there is a growing suspicion that we are mere receivers of a "creation of events" imposed by the large media that have the power to set the agenda.'
F. Matta[5]

Here is the News . . .

In Britain more than sixteen million viewers a day tune into BBC or ITV to watch the main evening news bulletins.

Satellite channels offer world news twenty-four hours a day. Over fourteen million people buy a newspaper. An IBA survey revealed that ninety-nine per cent of the population look to TV, radio and the press as the main source of information about the world in which they live. Day by day we witness accidents and disasters, we visit Northern Ireland, the stock exchange, the White House, parliament, the Brandenberg Gate and Red Square. Their importance and significance is explained. The implications of the latest advance in technology, the most recent coup, a rise in interest rates, the balance of trade deficit and falling share prices are spelled out. The news media expose us to the world which lies beyond the confines of our humdrum daily experience. They explain how it works. They provide information for concern and for complacency, for international anxiety and for national pride. They help us to see our place in a confusing and confused society.

Governments are keenly aware of the effect that news images can have. When American television showed pictures of their troops destroying the homes of innocent peasants in Vietnam, being out-manoeuvred and beaten by a guerrilla army enjoying wide popular support, President Johnson accused them of betraying their country. To this day, many observers maintain that the nightly TV news bulletins caused the 'collapse of American morale'. By undermining popular support for the war at home they helped to bring about the political climate which led to the eventual American withdrawal. The Ministry of Defence heeded the lesson. When Britain went to war in the Falklands in 1982, reports were subject to the strictest censorship and TV pictures of the fighting and British wounded were prevented from reaching Britain until after victory was assured. The almost 'live' coverage of a prime-ministerial visit a few weeks later provided a startling contrast.

At election time, prospective MPs and rival party leaders jostle for a place on the evening news. They are advised by teams of 'media specialists' who help them project the 'right' image. They set up special events to provide telegenic opportunities. Even the Church is beginning to wake up to the importance of news images. The Church of England is developing a national network of full- and part-time press, publicity, and communications officers whose job is not only to respond to media interest, but to 'project' images of its life.[6]

Ed Murrow, the legendary American newscaster, used to end his broadcasts with the words: 'And that's the way it is . . . ' A bold assertion. But how does what we read in the papers and see on television compare with 'the way it is'? What do newspapers and news broadcasts actually tell us about the world? How are their pictures and images constructed? And what do they contribute to social life? Even if the news media do not *control* our thoughts, actions and reflections on the world, their selection and presentation help to set an agenda for public debate. Their choice about what is important and what will be featured, controls 'the crucial information with which we are to make up our minds about the world.'[7]

For Christians, news images are especially important. Sunday by Sunday Christians pray, not only for their own needs, but for the wider needs 'of the Church and the world'. Our prayers and concerns cannot be limited by our immediate experience, but extend to all areas of life. Like everybody else, our impression of those 'needs' is largely derived from the media.

The Christian faith is not a 'Sunday-only' religion – it lays a wider claim to our daily lives. Our lives become expressions of our Christian principles. The way we live depends as much on our understanding of the world as of the Bible. For example, a common Christian concern for the sanctity and dignity of human life may lead one Christian to support anti-apartheid movements in South Africa and another a parliamentary lobby for a bill designed to limit the availability of abortions. The ways we choose to bear witness to the Gospel are determined by a number of factors: our understanding of the Christian faith, our personal experience, but also, to a large extent, by our perception of the key problems and issues which confront us. It is that perception which is in large part determined by the images that the news media provide.

Over the past 100-150 years, print and broadcast news in the western democracies have seen themselves as a vital support to democratic public decision-making. Journalists have assumed the role of the 'Fourth estate', the watchdog of government. During the 'Spycatcher' debacle newspapers and courts defended the principle that the public's right to know outweighs the loyalty an employee owes to the government of the day. They have protested about legislation to strengthen privacy laws and restrict access to information. 'Balance' and 'objectivity' are enshrined in the BBC charter. Fair, accurate and impartial news produced by free and independent news media is seen to be vital to a free and independent democracy.[8] After the fall of Ceausescu, news bulletins offered us images of a new 'free' Romania – citizens reading the first editions of a new free press.

But current research on news-making brings these ideals into question. Perhaps the snippets of information on the evening news obscure rather than illumine reality? Perhaps they cover over deeper issues and create merely the illusion of being informed? Media attention to the famine in Africa in 1984, whilst providing a focus for public attention and compassion for the *victims* of famine, did little to raise awareness of the political and economic causes which lay behind it and nothing to bring about an end to the Ethiopian conflict or prevent a recurrence in 1990.[9]

Although there are examples of deliberate attempts to mislead, many more studies have highlighted the subtle, systematic distortion of public reality inherent in today's news production and content.[10] Those who work in the news media are still motivated by the illusory ideal of 'objectivity'.[11] The brave, lonely reporter searching doggedly for the 'truth', fending off all attempts to pervert and obscure reality – contending with those who have a vested interest in promoting their own partial and distorted

view – is still a popular 'folk' image. It is a world away
from the experience of anyone who has stood back and
studied the way that news is 'produced'. It will not convince those who are shocked by the contrast between their
own experience of an event and the subsequent images
which have appeared in the media. Their anecdotes are
confirmed by systematic, extensive and elaborate studies
of news images. They suggest that the way in which news
is selected and presented accounts for it being so often
'out of focus'.

Man Bites Dog!

News is often presented as something which stands out
from everyday reality; something 'newsworthy'. This is
misleading. It belies the systematic and routine way in
which news is portrayed. Studies which have examined
a range of issues in the press, radio and television have
found that the events which are reported conform to certain accepted 'news values'.[12] The more of these a story
contains – the more likely it is to become 'news'. Disaster,
conflict, controversy, violence, change and dramatic rever-
sals – events which threaten stability and order are certain
to become news.[13] Stories feature famous people, they are
personalised, they recount bizarre or strange events, they
appear dramatic and simple and, most importantly, they can
usually draw on readily available, authoritative sources to
explain their importance and significance – politicians, the
police, trade union leaders, academics and studio experts.
Together they feed the news media's voracious appetite and
their 'innocent urge to entertain'.[14]

   One of the principal effects of this selection and presentation is an overall lack of explanation. Whereas one-
off events and unusual happenings conform to these news
values, issues do not. 'Disputes are reported, solutions pass
unnoticed. British newspapers are at their best when faced
with events moving quickly towards a dramatic climax,'[15]

as in eastern Europe in late 1989. In concentrating on an event, explanation is quickly lost. For example, a study of the way news about the women's movement was presented found that it was transformed in its early stages into novelty news such as 'bra-burning' or other 'soft' news, an entertaining curiosity rather than an issue to be seriously debated. Once the women's movement became hard news, it was presented in terms of the superficial journalistic narrative, telling the who, what, where, without getting at the reasons behind the event. Similarly, attempts to understand the issues and conditions which lie behind news about social policy are submerged beneath a welter of political and criminal events.[16] Daily news bulletins produce a limited range of discrete elements. They largely obscure the social processes which lie behind them.[17]

But although events may be wrenched from their wider social context, the media do offer their viewers, listeners and readers ways to interpret them – that after all is part of their job. First, stories are often compared with previous or similar events. These then provide an initial 'frame' which effectively shapes the way in which news about a current event is presented.[18] Protest action by nurses and a strike at Ford early in 1988 were seen by some media as the beginnings of widespread industrial anarchy – the dawn of another 'winter of discontent'. Comparisons and parallels are drawn between industrial disputes.

Second, the media also give space to those 'qualified' to offer interpretation and comment. They readily reproduce the understanding of those who can offer swift, reliable and authoritative comment – MPs for political topics, employers and trade union leaders for industrial matters, organised interest groups, bishops and Christian politicians, accredited experts and so on. These views, perceptions and opinions effectively set the limit for all subsequent discussion by framing what the problem is. Once an initial framework is set, it provides the criteria by which all subsequent contributors are labelled as 'relevant' to the debate, or 'irrelevant' – beside the point.[19]

Studies of news reports have repeatedly shown that some interest groups 'set the scene' more often than others. Employers rather than unions, government rather than oppositional interest groups, the police rather than demonstrators, striking miners or travellers on their way to an informal pop festival. This not only colours the way events are presented, it also acts as an important filter in the selection of news items. News about social policy is a typical example. Issues are framed and the disputes lined up by the discourse and consensus of Westminster and Whitehall.

Although there are some examples which suggest that Westminster does not always set the agenda – there was much public sympathy for the ambulance workers during their pay dispute in 1990, and the poll-tax was not generally viewed by most voters as being fairer than the rating system it replaced – they tend to be exceptions to a pronounced trend. The production of policy rather than its impact on claimants dominates news about the social security system. Consequently, the social security system is presented as an expensive administrative problem, a burden borne by 'us' (the public – the readers and viewers), imposed by 'them' (the spenders of our taxes) to support other people. Real human problems (the focus of this administration and expenditure) receive little exposure in relation to the measures employed to contain or solve them.[20] Where they do, they become isolated incidents.

Those who are granted space to define the initial conflict have a key role in shaping total coverage of an event. Later coverage tends to conform to their definitions and interpretations.

In spite of the way the news media present a world made up of 'random' events and concentrate on 'unusual' occurrences, their largely uniform presentation helps to generate and reinforce a common social ideology. They re-circulate a common stock of 'taken-for-granted' knowledge that presents society as a special order which is made up of movement but not innovation. They stress that society is basically stable and assert the existence of a commonly shared set of assumptions. Their definitions coincide with and reinforce an essential social consensus.[21] They invite us not only to see their world as 'the way it is', but also 'the way it *should* be'.

Other studies of news content have pointed out that important issues and problems are mis-represented by this systematic portrayal. Once a framework for debate has been set, the media *exclude* interpretations and views which fall outside it. While certain points of view are ignored, others are highlighted and reinforced. For example, a study of the way 'Faith in the City' was covered by the press showed that, although the report was given an unusually high profile, media coverage revolved around accusations that the report was 'Marxist', 'confused' and leaked to the press. The underlying issues which prompted the Church commission – the problem of the inner cities – received scant attention and were largely obscured by the political storm which anticipated and attended its publication.[22]

News which is framed to conform to established perceptions and presented according to set 'news values' gives a systematic distortion to 'the way it is . . . ' It reaffirms an ideological framework which persistently repeats consensual values. It effectively 'reifies' and treats as objective fact the current social order, with all its divisions and conflicts. Its claim to be 'trustworthy' and 'balanced' and to present an objective, impartial reality makes its contribution both subtle and powerful.

But why is it this way? How is this 'systematic distortion' produced? How can these studies of news products be reconciled with the high ideals and dedication of those who work in the media?

Making the News

Studies suggest that journalists and editors often consciously apply 'news values' when they select and report stories. Studies have found that news images of the Church have a particular skew.[23] The preoccupation with moral conflict and internal division may be less a feature of Church life and more a product of the media's skewed attention to division and the bizarre. Similarly news about the social security system was seen by journalists as 'intrinsically boring' and needed to be 'seasoned with drama, language and values of the entertainment media that the modern news service has become'. It only ever 'surfaces in its more flamboyant or "grabby" form'.[24] After Derek Deevey was convicted of obtaining up to £500 in supplementary benefit by deception in 1976, the press was awash not only with unsubstantiated claims of widespread social security fraud – but also of apparent 'legal largesse' of 'cigars and drinks and a good tax-free life for bums' (*Daily Express* 16.8.76) supported by the 'honest' tax-payer!

Journalists do not only see life as a repertoire of events, some of which contain the necessary 'ingredients' for a successful news story, they go on to 'season' and dramatise other events with the same ingredients. In 1989, tabloid newspaper stories of homeless teenagers on the streets in London largely revolved around the spurious claims by the *Sun* that a fortune could be made from begging on the Underground. Newspapers (if not the streets) were soon awash with journalists disguised as beggars, reckoning up a day's takings. The real issues of London street life – poverty, homelessness, and the inevitable slide into prostitution, were largely ignored.

But stories can also be affected by a journalist's own values and experiences.[25] For example, some studies of religious news have suggested that this may be a significant factor in the way that the Church is portrayed.[26] Also, individual racist attitudes and too few female staff may explain why women and minority racial groups are under-represented in news stories.[27] Individual journalist's attitudes are undoubtedly an additional contributory factor. However, they cannot explain the *systematic* distortion that long-term studies have exposed – nor how similar distortions occur in different cultures and environments.[28]

Recent research into the way news is produced has focused on the unintended but systematically biased view of the world that results from routine, accepted practices of news gathering and the bureaucratic structure of news organisations. Studies of news gatherers have confronted the 'news men's mythology' that news is largely 'the product of a lack of organisation' and have highlighted the routine. News producers are subject to 'a variety of constraints erected by the routines of work, of news gathering and production and by deliberate and regular interventions, conspiratorial or otherwise, of those with axes to grind and the muscle to do so effectively'.[29] These constraints fall into two categories.

The first of these is *financial*. The work of a journalist is affected by the needs of technology and by the need to be profitable within a budget.[30] Corporate policy and internal budgetary requirements play their part in shaping the direction of television news. News departments exist within wider broadcast organisations and are in competition for its resources – as mundane as whether a film crew is available or not.[31] When the fog descends on the north west, camera crews are so busy covering the resulting motorway carnage that viewers of regional news magazines could be forgiven for thinking that nothing else has happened that day! Selection of news is made from what is accessible. Coverage of foreign news is often criticised for giving a particularly distorted view of events. This follows a reduction in specialist foreign correspondents and an increasing dependence on the four major international agencies, who collect and distribute the same stories, interviews and pictures to different news organisations. Within the press, competition between different specialist departments is often finally decided by their capacity to generate advertising revenue.[32]

The second constraint is produced by the *working environment* of journalists. Broadcast journalism is not the random reaction to random events that many people think. On the contrary, it is a highly regulated and routine process which manufactures a cultural product on an electronic production line. 'In stages of planning, gathering, selection and production, broadcast news is moulded by the demands of composing order and organisation within a daily cycle. The news is made, and like any other product it carries the marks of the technical and organisational structure from which it emerges.'[33] The problem is further compounded by the media dependence upon other sources of news. TV newsrooms are awash with other newspapers. Newspaper offices are alert to radio and TV bulletins. The media feed off themselves. 'Faith in the City' – the 1985 report of the Archbishop of Canterbury's Commission on Urban Priority Areas – was first 'broken' in a Church paper in the north east and then picked up by a stringer working for a London daily.

This bureaucratic and largely routine nature of news production is further enhanced by broadcasters' and journalists' dependence on bureaucratic and routine sources. As one analyst commented: 'Even . . . stories about the local area, forests and wildlife depended upon the forestry service for its news. When it turned out that even rocks, trees, and squirrels are made available to the newspaper through official agencies, then it is no exaggeration to say that the world is bureaucratically organised for journalists.'[34]

Public bureaucracies often develop a symbiotic relationship with the news media. For the journalist, these bureaucracies represent a reliable and authoritative source of news items. In their turn, the bureaucracies are able to use the news media to project and promote views and opinions sympathetic to their cause. The centralised, legitimated institutions – government offices, public services and corporate headquarters – which regularly make news available to the media can thereby ensure that a steady supply of partially assembled data or pseudo 'media' events already bears their official interpretation.

Whilst sources cannot determine *which* news stories are used and what images and values the media will finally convey, they certainly help to focus journalists' attention. The values, interpretations and 'ways of seeing the world' that they contain are part of the 'information' they provide. For example, the fact that politicians are almost invariably the source for news about social welfare means that *their* understanding, definition and solutions to the 'problems' are the ones reflected by the media. The 'problem' of so-called social security scroungers (beloved by certain populist newspapers) is in reality dwarfed by the much deeper problem of those who cannot understand the benefit system, and are unable to take advantage of the support to which they are entitled. Yet this problem is rarely the focus of concern of politicians or government departments. It rarely surfaces in the news.[35]

The reliance upon accredited, institutional spokespeople (and the consequent projection of their ways of seeing the world) is paradoxically reinforced by a news organisation's quest for 'objectivity' and their avowed desire to present a 'balanced' picture. A television or press report will often seek out people who can provide a countervailing point of view – government and opposition spokespeople, employees and trade unionists, conservative and liberal Churchmen etc. In replying to the first, the opposition necessarily reinforces the parameters and terms of the first – their comments would not appear relevant otherwise. A politician who was asked for his solution to the problem of social security 'scroungers', would seem to be avoiding the issue if he spoke instead about those who failed to take up benefit. The politician's charge that 'Faith in the City' was 'Marxist' and 'inspired by communist clerics' was answered by Church commentators that it could not be construed as Marxist, that it was 'carefully researched' etc. This shifted the whole focus of newspaper coverage. Instead of discussing inner-city conditions and the problems and opportunities they presented to the Church and nation, newspapers, politicians and Church leaders discussed whether the Marxist tag was justified, whether the Church should involve itself in politics, how the report was leaked etc. The term 'Marxist' may have eventually been discredited but its early use effectively shifted the focus of debate. Discussion of the Commission's proposals hardly materialised. Few people would have gained any idea of the substance of the report from reading their newspapers.[36]

Further, this 'bi-polar' objective is almost invariably conducted between institutional or accredited sources. As well as balancing opposing views, the media try to use oppositional spokespeople of equivalent authority. Whilst the government and senior Church personnel debated 'Faith in the City' on television and in the press, very little attention was given to those who lived and worked in the inner cities! Similarly most Church news in Britain is news about the Church of England. Bishops in the House of Lords offer a ready supply of suitably recognisable, authoritative, and colourful spokespeople.

News organisations become highly amenable to skilful manipulation and careful news management by the very sources upon which they are so dependent. Whereas the parliamentary lobby system was originally established to provide more open information for journalists, many have seen it fulfil the opposite role in recent years. One journalist describes it as 'a party to government news management'.[37] Often the state or its official agencies are the only sources to which journalists have access (as with the early US reports of the Vietnam war, and British government handling of the Falklands conflict, Northern Ireland or the security services). This allows them complete control of information. They can effectively 'feed' journalists with selected stories.

Sometimes journalists are willing participants in attempts to shape the public agenda.[38] Occasionally, examples of covert attempts by governments and bureaucracies to 'manipulate' the news come to light. By their very nature they are rare and it is impossible to establish whether they are the exception or the rule. More common is the carefully timed release of information which may be embarrassing, or its 'upstaging' by other events. In March, 1990, Britain announced its 'clean-up' programme of the North Sea – just ahead of a conference at which it was roundly condemned for failure to do anything effective about sewage and effluent dumping.

It is, rather, the routine way in which news is gathered and produced that best enables the government and other powerful bureaucracies to influence how it is presented. Media dependence upon representatives of the state as primary sources of news and comment means that news organisations are virtually obliged to transmit the state's definitions of a situation. It is this feature which tends to reify it and make it appear objective. The state is able to set a definition which is likely to underpin all subsequent reporting.[39]

By looking behind the surface at both the content of our daily 'news' and the way that it is produced, researchers have built up a picture of news which is characterised by distortion, avoidance of issues, unequal access and the state's capacity to set the agenda for public debate. This is not 'the way it is . . . ' but one of many ways of looking at the world – one which inevitably and invariably reflects the interests and perceptions of the power élites in society. The news media are not simply transparent windows through which we view the world. They are part and parcel of that world – as much shaped by it as they are influential in shaping our perceptions of it. 'Media themselves are often referred to as a "mirror of society" . . . This mirror, of course, is clouded, giving us less-than-perfect reflections of our human selves, individually and collectively.'[40]

In order to penetrate and challenge the beguilingly simple façade that the news offers it is important for Christians:

First, *to look behind its images and stories* to evaluate not only *what* is said and done, but the *way* it is shown. Why have they been selected? Whose interests are served by telling them in this way? A more critical awareness of the way that news is produced and received will enable us to develop an immunity to unwittingly absorbing the popular definitions that news stories enshrine.

Second, *to take seriously and listen to those who have a different understanding and perceptions of events*. The media offer just some of the many possible ways of looking at the world. Others which may be just as valid are often hidden by the routine processes of news production. Had the crucifixion been reported by the mass media, we would doubtless have read some interesting and accurate accounts of events in the Jewish and Roman press. But, if we'd been able to find them, Jesus's own 'criminal' friends would probably have told a very different tale.

Third, *to support alternative news networks.* Christians in the third world are beginning to realise that one way they can challenge the way that news and information currently serve dominant interests is by setting up their own independent news and information networks (the Inter Press Service and Interdoc). The content of information can then be determined by the context of the poor, oppressed and marginalised. But even these have their problems. In order to survive, IPS has to exist as a commercial news agency. There are real problems in trying to explain the context and process behind an event in the bite-sized 300-word pieces beloved by western media consumers. In western, industrial democracies community broadsheets, newspapers and radio stations are attempting the same thing – to offer ordinary people news and information that is relevant to their immediate needs. If local churches are serious about meeting the needs of the communities they serve, they need to encourage, support and participate in such initiatives – to begin to take and disseminate news from these 'alternative' sources.

Fourth, *to resist pressure to reproduce the same patterns of news 'distortion' in 'Church' news and information.* Do parish and diocesan news channels reflect the perceptions and interests of local church élites and committees rather than the people they serve? How far does national Church news reflect the understanding of an ecclesiastical hierarchy rather than the everyday concerns of ordinary Christians? How many clergy who complain in private about the volume and irrelevance of much of their monthly diocesan mailing perpetuate the same sin in their parish communications?

Many of those who watch, read, work in or study the media are unhappy with the way that 'news' is defined and presented. 'It will not change until the population who are mis-represented and who suffer the effects of bad news, demand instead truly democratic media.'[41]

Chapter Seven

The medium or the message?
Religious Broadcasting

' . . . the traditional churches have shown, from the very earliest days of broadcasting, an absolutely *underwhelming* interest in the media.'

S. Hoover[1]

'Perhaps religious broadcasting . . . is destined to be dominated by independent swashbuckling entrepreneurs . . . '

P. Elvy[2]

'In broadcasting systems where religious programming is defined as a public service . . . religious programmes . . . are more of a sociological debate than an expression of religious faith.'

R. White[3]

'The religious broadcaster is confronted by an absurdity – trying to proclaim from a position of immense secular power the futility of secular power compared to the divine strength exhibited in utter weakness on the cross . . . like a millionaire preaching the virtues of poverty from the back seat of a gold-plated Rolls!'

C. Morris[4]

In 1923, John Reith, the young general manager of the newly formed British Broadcasting Company, invited Archbishop Randall Davidson and his wife to dinner. During the evening he switched on the 'wireless'. Schubert's 'March Militaire' filled the room. Dr Davidson was 'thunderstruck'. He saw at once that this new invention offered the Churches enormous communications potential. The very next day he called together Church leaders to discuss the possibilities of the new medium.

Many were indifferent and did not share Dr Davidson's view. But John Reith was a devout Christian and firmly believed that 'If the Churches recognise their new opportunity, there will not be room enough to hold their people!'[5] His vision was shared, developed and brought to life by pioneer religious broadcasters. Under their vision and guidance, as the new medium evolved, religion became an integral part of it.

Over the last sixty years, many landmarks have been and gone: the first television transmission, the introduction of commercial television, local and commercial radio, a fourth television channel, satellite and cable systems. Religious broadcasting has so far weathered the storm. Through formal links with the media, (the Central Religious Advisory Committee, the Churches Advisory Committee for Local Broadcasting, and the British Churches Committee for Channel 4), and through other less formal contacts, the institutional Church has shared in the way that religious broadcasting has been able to develop and adapt to new communications environments. As broadcasting moves into a world of cable, satellite, community radio and 'de-regulated' national broadcasting heralded by the 1990 Broadcasting Act, the Churches are seeking to continue their partnership with the media; through these formal bodies, through their responses to government proposals, and above all through the good will, integrity and ministry of Christians who work in the media.

But a partnership depends on the willing commitment of both sides. Whilst the Churches are committed to the idea of religious broadcasting, the 'new' media may not be so keen.

Religious broadcasting was originally offered a place on

the 'ether' by John Reith. It has maintained its privileged position for a number of reasons.

1. The public service philosophy, which has been the cornerstone of British broadcasting policy, sees broadcasting as a service to the whole community. Its task is to address all groups in society regardless of status or purchasing power. Reith saw its threefold function to 'educate, inform and entertain'. Churchgoers represent a significant sector of society, an identifiable audience, who can legitimately expect to find their interests catered for by a public broadcast system, as can lovers of classical or jazz music. The Church is also the object of interest of a media system which seeks to 'inform and educate' its wider audience. A recent study which looked at the image of religion that the media present found that most references to religion occurred *outside* what could be legitimately regarded as religious broadcasts, in current affairs, news and entertainment media (even sports programmes had their share!).[6] A public service broadcast system will cover religion simply because it is there!

2. The Church has also maintained a special relationship with the media because the leaders and senior 'professionals' of both institutions are largely drawn from a common stratum of society. They share common interests, opinions and views of the world. Both are similar products of the British class system, were educated in the same way and trained together to be 'balanced and objective'.[7] Indeed a much publicised recent criticism of the Anglican hierarchy drew attention to this very connection.[8] The BBC and Church of England also display similar institutional characteristics. Both are national institutions largely funded by 'other people's money', both attempt to preserve a semblance of isolation from direct government interference. Both are somehow distinctly 'British'.

3. The bureaucracy of media organisations finds a natural counterpart in the traditional Church. Many studies have shown how easily the media relate to other bureaucratic organisations.[9] The Church can provide authoritative, socially acceptable figures to provide comment and reflection. The views of 'the Church' (some thirteen per cent of the adult population) can often be summed up and represented by a cleric in a dog collar easily reached through the broadcasting department at Church House (who will even ensure that he is telegenic!).

4. If the media naturally gravitate to a bureaucratic Church, so the Church, with a message to proclaim, is naturally interested in any system of communication. St Paul found himself drawn to the Roman market (Acts 17:17–18) – the hub of social life where gossip, news and entertainment were to be found, where ideas and philosophies were exchanged, where justice was seen to be done.[10] If the Church is to be taken seriously today, it needs to set up its stall in the current 'market place' of gossip, news and entertainment – the mass media. For that is where the twentieth century sets out its philosophies and ideas and where justice is seen to be done.

5. Finally, Christianity is a 'world-affirming' faith. The Church has always declared (although its actions have often failed to live up to its intentions) that the world, created by God, is *de facto* an object of Christian concern and attention. Christians have responded to Christ's call to be 'salt in the world' by making a contribution to society and culture at an institutional and individual level: through those whose work is an expression of Christian concern (chaplains in hospitals, prisons etc, Christian charities and relief organisations, groups which campaign for justice and human rights) and through the lives of ordinary Christians who try to live out their faith at work. Gerald Priestland once said that what the Church should be concerned with was not producing more Christian broadcasts but more Christian broadcasters!

But where has this natural affinity led? Reith's expectation of religious broadcasting heralding a new religious revival is largely unfulfilled. Many have seen exactly the opposite – that in spite of a recognisable Christian presence, the media have played a key role in creating a secular society – a social environment in which churches are turned into concert halls and night-clubs and where 'religion' plays an ever-diminishing role. The analysis from America – from those who live in a very different communications environment and experience a very different style of religious broadcasting – is harsh. What else can you expect? they ask, Godless state broadcasting is bound to produce a Godless state. Religious broadcasters have become the unwitting servants of the secular institutions they serve. They have failed to deliver the goods. Are they right?

Religion and Public Service Broadcasting

As we have seen earlier, television and radio are not the simple 'windows onto the world' that some advocates have claimed. The images that they bring into our homes are the end result of a complicated, routinised production process. At one level, these images are partly the creation of the medium itself. For example, TV inevitably deals in stereotypes; it concentrates on events rather than issues, on personalities rather than principles, on controversy rather than consensus. It feeds on immediate, fast-moving events which generate good pictures. That means a peaceful on-going protest is unlikely to hit the headlines: a violent demonstration is. A vicar saving souls, quietly serving his parochial flock is unlikely to make the news, even on local radio. A tap-dancing curate, knitting bishop, Sunday school centenary or bishop running in the London marathon – well that's another story.

But the content of a programme, and the values it embodies, are coloured as much by the circumstances in which it is produced as by the subject matter or format of the medium. Religious programmes do not exist in a political and economic vacuum. They are part of a much wider broadcast system. Before the 1990 Broadcasting Act, British religious broadcasting developed its particular content and style as part of a public service broadcast system. The air-waves belonged to all people. Those who broadcast, whether on the BBC or commercial channels, were responsible to the public as a whole rather than to any particular segment or group.

Although there have been some who have defended the right of a public service to be used as an evangelistic tool[11], the early pioneers of religious broadcasting saw that this could create immense problems for a public service. If the established religions and main Christian denominations were allowed to proselytise over the air-waves – then so should minority groups such as Jehovah's Witnesses, Mormons, Unitarians etc. Religious broadcasts, far from presenting the highest ideals of the Christian faith, would simply become a cacophony. Groups would compete with one another. The air-waves would become just another forum for the division and dissent that had blighted the Churches' mission for two thousand years. Instead, religious broadcasting gained the respect of broadcasters, the mainstream Churches and the public by becoming an adjunct to the Churches' ministry. It sought to express commonly shared Christian values rather than the particular beliefs or opinions of any group or denomination. It was seen as a way of encouraging listeners to think about their faith and to relate it to everyday life. It became a means by which the Church, and indeed the whole nation, could become 'informed' and 'educated' about developments in the life, theology and witness of the Churches.

In 1977, the Central Religious Advisory Committee, an ecumenical panel that advised the broadcast organisations on religious policy, tried to re-formulate these broad objectives. Religious broadcasting, they said, should:

1. seek to reflect the worship, thought and action of the principal religious foundations represented in Britain, recognising that the traditions are mainly, though not exclusively, Christian;

2. seek to present to viewers and listeners those beliefs, ideas, issues and experiences in the contemporary world as are evidently related to a religious interpretation or dimension of life;

3. seek also to meet the religious interests, concerns and needs of those on the fringe of, or outside the organised life of, the churches.

The programme formats that have become a feature of broadcast departments reflect this public-service commitment to a broad appeal – televised services, community hymn singing, religious current-affairs documentaries, thought and comment for the day, religious 'news' magazines and, more recently, devotional and contemplative explorations of religious themes. But the system under which a programme is made affects much more than its format. It colours the content as well.

Local commercial radio provides a good working example of how broadcasting structure determines the shape of a programme. Commercial operators are granted an advertising monopoly in exchange for a commitment to provide a *local* radio service, broadcasting news and features generated in, or relevant to, its listeners. At the same time, in order to satisfy the needs of their advertisers and shareholders, they have to attract the largest audience possible at the lowest cost. The involvement of local Christians enables them to fulfil their local obligation and to meet an IBA requirement to provide religious programmes at little additional cost. That these programmes can satisfy these dual requirements is testimony to the dedication and professionalism of any such 'part-time' religious broadcasters. In fact a study of London's commercial radio output found that their religious features were practically the only time when local people were heard!

But religious broadcasts also have to be integrated with a commercial station's need to maximise advertising revenue. The familiar diet of popular music, lively advertisements and inconsequential chat by 'transatlantic' DJs is the undemanding, commonly accepted formula which achieves the high ratings that advertisers demand. These requirements have produced the commercial-radio 'religious magazine' in which Church 'items' punctuate the music like advertisements. To those who have no Church affiliation, (perhaps the majority of listeners) they present an amorphous picture of the Church. Religious life is expressed in bulletins and short snippets of information, consisting of a succession of curious clerics, jumble sales, parties and special events, centenary services, book reviews, numerous 'activities' and passing dignitaries who 'pop' in to the studio. The structural and financial imperatives which control commercial broadcasting mean that religious reality is presented in convenient, part-digested, 'bite-sized' pieces. The outlandish, 'dramatic' and unusual features of Church life are persistently highlighted. The daily adventure of Christian living is necessarily ignored.

The BBC are not immune from such commercial pressures. Religious programmes have to compete with other programmes for a place in the schedules if the BBC is to achieve ratings high enough to justify its claim to the licence fee. The writing may be on the wall for programmes catering for minority tastes – religious programmes amongst them.[12]

In a study of the way in which religion was portrayed in the media, Kim Knott concludes that, as a result of these structural pressures, religious broadcasting has become 'standardised and featureless'. It has had to accommodate itself to conform to the values inherent in the media system. It has had to blend with its surroundings.

In an attempt to move with the times, to respond to the seemingly inevitable process of secularisation, religious broadcasting has abandoned much of what made it distinctive. We can observe that the roles and functions of religious broadcasting – to inform and guide, to give comfort and help – have become the content of religious programmes . . . Christian belief and practice, though retained in Sunday morning televised services and evening hymn-singing programmes, often take second place to programmes that discuss moral choices, that depict the Church and its ministers in their social roles, that offer advice and canvass help. This is undeniably useful and important. What it is not is distinctive . . . The religious character of religious television has often been forfeited . . . with the result that it has now become no different to other television output.[13]

The religious broadcasts we have in Britain today, and consequently the image of the Church that they present, are largely the result of the demands of the communication system in which they exist. Whilst these draw heavily on the tradition of public service broadcasting, the new competitive age heralded by the 1990 Broadcasting Act and the new demands of commercial competition are beginning to make their mark. The religious needs of the viewers and listeners, the theological perspectives of the Churches, even insights from current mass communication theory about the way people absorb, respond to, and 'use' media images contribute little by comparison.

The Commercial Alternative

American religious broadcasts are the product of a very different communications environment, which developed in response to a very different tradition. In a country where 'the free market and free speech are both articles of Faith' the mass media were (in theory) open to all who wished to enter.[14] In 1925, whilst the BBC was still in its infancy, there were some sixty-three American stations owned by Church institutions. However, early Church interest soon diminished as the limited radio spectrum meant that wavelengths became a scarce commodity – only available to the highest bidder. Commercial operators soon took over the stations. Following the 1935 Communications Act, religious broadcasts were granted 'grace and favour' status on the networks. At the same time, many small denominations and religious groups, were frustrated by what they saw as mainline protestant domination of network broadcasting. They purchased air-time on the plethora of local stations. The balance of 'free' and 'paid-for' air-time steadily shifted.

When more UHF TV frequencies became available in the 'sixties, the radio evangelists took the opportunity to move into television. But the biggest fillip to the electronic Church (as it has become known) has been signalled by 'a spirit of de-regulation'. Until 1970 the Federal Communications Commission had acted as watchdog (albeit without any effective teeth!) to restrain all-out commercial interest and preserve a place for religious and public interest programmes in the commercial stations. It monitored their accounts and, like the ITC, set criteria that operators had to meet. In 1970 it stated that a station could serve its public interest just as well with religious programmes that had been 'bought in'. With their obligation to provide free air-time removed, the networks provided fewer facilities and opportunities for the Churches. By 1977 'paid-for' religious television accounted for ninety-two per cent of American religious air-time. And, as voluntary institutions, religious organisations enjoy immunity from even the FCC's cursory financial oversight. The field was set for televangelist Jim Bakker's much publicised trial for fraud and financial malpractice.

Just as the British system has produced its own genre of media religion and projected certain facets of Church life, so the US experience of de-regulation has led to a certain kind of religious broadcast. The financial demands of purchasing more time, running bigger TV stations, using satellites and computer technology to reach ever greater numbers of viewers has produced its own image of the Church. Pressure to compete as popular entertainment media has led the US electronic churches to imitate the successful formulae of commercial television – a TV 'magazine'

show, with a succession of successful media 'stars' to emulate; Christian news and games shows; even Christian soap
opera. Their message has to be equally as attractive. They
have to make their viewers feel good (if not they tune
to another channel). Electronic Christianity has shared,
contributed to and developed new expressions of personal
acquisition – and all these ideas have to be turned into
cash if they are to survive. 'Both motivation theory and
pragmatism born of experience in religious broadcasting dic-
tate that the greatest promise of benefit elicits the greatest
response . . . TV preachers may begin with the simplest and
sincerest of motives, but they are inevitably confronted with
the budget demands of producing programmes, building
colleges or cathedrals and paying for the escalating costs
of broadcasting time'.[15]

Although it may be hard when viewing the end result to
discern the common stock of two such divergent modes of
religious expression, religious broadcasting in both Britain
and America is the product of Church accommodation,
integration and compromise to two very different and distinctive media delivery systems.

Change is Coming[16]

Whatever the relative merits of the two broadcast systems
(they share a common sympathy for each other's victims!)
broadcasting as we know it in Britain is changing radically.
The concept of public service broadcasting, founded on the
principle that the air-waves belong to the people, has come
to an end. Competitive commercial broadcasting in which
control, finance and, ultimately, content is handed over to
private hands is the road down which Britain and much
of Europe is heading. In the 1990 Broadcasting Act the
government proposes to expand commercial broadcasting
and drastically limit its public service requirement whilst
putting a financial squeeze on the BBC. It argues that the
BBC, Channel 4 and the new tier of commercially funded

'community' radio stations will become the last refuge of public service broadcasting. The public will be better served by more stations competing for their attention.

At the same time, private companies and multi-national entertainment corporations are eager to exploit the potential new advertising and electronics markets that the new generation of direct broadcast satellites will offer. BSkyB – Britain's first commercial satellite channel – hopes that the satellite dishes needed to receive their programmes will soon become as commonplace as the television aerial. Viewers will be able to choose from a plethora of new television channels. The government hope that the new channels will lead to increased programme choice. This flies in the face of existing evidence which suggests that competition in the media encourages imitative rather than innovative broadcasting, and multiplicity rather than variety. In America, pop music, films, repeats, the news and weather forecasts have become the staple fare of the most successful and profitable channels. Critics point out that 'as soon as the possibility of making a profit is put on the agenda, the concept of public service broadcasting disintegrates'.[17] The real consumers of this new 'competitive' age will not be the viewers, but the advertisers who purchase their attention. The viewers become the commodity which is bought and sold. Stewart Hoover sums up the American experience of 'lighter' regulation and seemingly increased choice: 'It has resulted in one of the best, most efficient systems ever known for delivering an audience. It has *not* provided and cannot provide a way to satisfy the public's demands'.[18]

If the regulatory system and organisational constraints under which a programme is made, affect its contents, style and, ultimately, the picture of 'reality' that it projects, any change to that system will have important repercussions. Colin Morris suggests that for many of the twenty million or so viewers and listeners that religious broadcasting currently attracts, television and radio is likely to represent their only contact with the Church.[19] As Britain (together with most of Europe) moves towards an American-style de-regulated/'free market' media system to take advantage of the new technology now available, religious broadcasting as we know it today will be transformed.

The Shape of Things to Come . . .

Star-gazing has its problems. The only thing we shall ever see by looking into a crystal ball is a distorted reflection of our own hopes and fears. On the other hand, an understanding of the way that media images are constructed and affected by the system in which they are produced, and a critical look at what has happened in countries which have already experienced some of the new technologies, allows us to make out the general shape of the future, even though its finer details must remain obscure.

First, we are likely to see the American TV evangelists broadcasting to Britain. After an exhaustive, first-hand detailed analysis of the American electronic Church, Peter Elvy confidently predicts that Europe is next on their list.[20] Many of the successful American televangelists are particularly eager to move into Britain, either by owning their own station, or by providing programmes for others. They see a new potential market for their TV shows. They view Britain as a dark, Godless island from whose air-waves the Gospel is effectively banished. Their entrepreneurial instincts have persuaded their viewers to part with billions of dollars, ostensibly to build hospitals, universities, grandiose glass mausoleums, to extend their 'successful' ministry, and to provide them with the trappings and material benefits suitable to a life 'blessed by God' (Cadillacs, private jets, country retreats etc). Who can doubt that their viewers will dig yet deeper into their pockets in order to provide funds to bring the Gospel to us poor benighted folks over the water! Some argue that legislation to prevent broadcasters appealing for funds over the air will protect Britain from the worst American excesses. But closer analysis suggests that this simple prohibition will not be enough. Many American channels use a phone/counselling line to establish initial contact. They later appeal for funds by direct mail.

The production facilities, the necessary satellite link-ups and even the programmes already exist. It will be far cheaper for them to 'break into' Europe than for European Church groups who will have to start from scratch. In the so-called 'free' media market, those who can purchase the most air time become the voices which are heard most often.

Second, any slimmed-down public service which continues to exist alongside the commercial ones will be unlikely to provide alternative styles of programmes. In order to justify a claim on the public purse, public service broadcasting will also have to compete for a sizeable share of the audience. The draught is already being felt in some BBC corridors.[21] The American experience has been that religious broadcasts – along with many other public interest programmes (children's, current affairs, social action, religion etc) – have been effectively squeezed from the schedules. The breath of fresh air which 'competition' is supposed to breathe into the BBC may well turn out to be a gale which slams shut the doors to its religious departments.

Third, a commercial system will not necessarily promote *effective* religious broadcasting. Programmes are likely to be evangelistic or ostensibly aimed at reaching 'new' Christians (some televangelists are able to produce incredibly inflated statistics to support their evangelistic claims).[22] But they have to satisfy the tastes, values and prejudices of those who provide the funds. These are either their *existing* viewers, or ecclesiastical bureaucrats whose good will and vision are needed to sustain and protect denominational broadcasting departments. Stewart Hoover exposes this paradox in his analysis of American mass media religion. Those who pay for the televangelists do so in the belief that the programmes reach a wholly fictitious audience of unbelievers.

. . . the content of the program is far less important to

these viewers than is the association of the program with their own communities of reference, with their social and cultural backgrounds, and with the dominant symbols and values of their worlds of meaning. This means that for most viewers, not only is Pat Robertson 'preaching to the choir' (in that his audience is already basically convinced), but that they are less interested in what he has to say than they are in associating the program with their other beliefs and involvements . . . They support it for 'those who really need it'. Realising that they themselves may actually be the typical or target audience of the program would belie its value for them.[23]

Fourth, the commercial success of the new channels will depend upon attracting significant numbers of regular viewers – either to pay subscriptions or to satisfy the needs of advertisers. Religious programmes will have to be integrated into the style and ethos of the new stations (in the same way that they currently 'merge' with public service or commercial channels). Religious broadcasting will have to mirror its secular counterparts and 'integrate every TV cliché, every technique of distraction, so that it will fit and people will not flick the channel knob in disgust'.[24] The values it promotes will have to be compatible with a philosophy of materialism and personal consumption which lies at the heart of commercial broadcasting.

Fifth, despite their stated aims and exaggerated figures, the evidence suggests that American-style TV evangelism preaches to the converted. Most committed, regular viewers are church members who watch more than one religious broadcast per week.[25] Like any other viewer, they will tend to select those programmes which reinforce the values and opinions they already hold. They may well be successful in offering some people comfort, hope and assurance, but only at the cost of sacrificing that part of the Christian Gospel which Jesus's listeners found an affront, challenging or disturbing. As one broadcaster himself put it ' . . . all that religious TV is doing is to make people feel good and to get them to keep on doing what they're doing!'[26]

If a commercial system is unable to produce programmes which will 'convert' the population of Britain, they are even less likely to enable existing Christians to develop, grow and mature.

New Contexts

As the shape and content of religious broadcasting changes, British Churches will find themselves ministering and proclaiming their message in new contexts and a different media market place.

1. A new theological context

The new de-regulated state broadcasting will present people with a highly entertaining and yet distinctly partial and distorted image of what commitment to Christ is all about. Horsfield sketches out the character of competitive TV religion as:

> 1. *Authoritative* It provides clear and unequivocal instruction on moral and religious problems.
>
> 2. *Individualistic* By stressing the individual as the foundational societal unit, the individual response of being born again becomes the Christian panacea for all social ills.
>
> 3. *Materialistic* It offers uncritical support for dominant social values, particularly material and consumptive ones.
>
> 4. *Paradoxical* It presents viewers with the paradox of seeing the world as transient and condemned and yet features guests whose material prosperity is a sign of their spiritual blessing.

If Colin Morris is right, and television *is* the only contact many have with the Church, who can blame them if it is all they ever want? Dr William Fore who, as assistant general secretary for the National Council of Churches of Christ in the USA, has had over thirty years' experience of living with the electronic Church concludes that whilst it does not represent a serious institutional threat to the mainline Churches, 'it does pose a threat to mainline theology . . . Their programmes consolidate and reinforce a restrictive and narrow view both of religion and the world.'[27]

2. A new political context

There have been many claims and counterclaims about the political impact of the American televangelists. Conservative, republican movements such as Jerry Falwell's 'Moral Majority' have not been slow to claim a significant role in the 1984 presidential elections. Serious analysts are more cautious. There is good evidence to suggest that the sort of people who are drawn to these religious programmes are already likely to support conservative proposals anyway.[28] What is beyond question, however, is that the personalised, authoritarian, materialistic gospel which televangelists proclaim (and which seems so suited to television), promotes the sorts of values which are necessary to maintain consumer societies. It is not hard to see why conservative political groups and wealthy industrialists are keen to endorse, support and encourage religious movements which support such values. The apparent success with which American televangelists have popularised such causes as anti-abortion, support for fascist dictatorships and military intervention in central America, increased defence spending, etc, will make their European counterparts similarly attractive to political groups in this country.

3. A new pastoral context

Commercial religious broadcasting will only exist if there are people to pay for it – and if there are people who want to watch it. The message of the electronic Church may largely confirm the prejudices of its small band of fanatical adherents and the religious indifference of casual viewers. It may appear distasteful, bland and a travesty of the Gospel to mainline Churches. But it has also shown itself extraordinarily adroit at reaching (and exploiting) many people who feel lonely and isolated in the modern world. These people find the established Churches 'dry, unfriendly, cold, dead or dying', whilst electronic Church ministers, whose only contact is through a television performance and computerised request for more money, are perceived as caring. 'The electronic Church succeeds primarily where we have failed,' comments one minister. 'Our pastoral ministries have been in large measure confined to a few parishioners, leaving vast numbers of aged, infirm and confined individuals groping for sympathetic companionship, personal faith and a sense of God's abiding presence.'[29] The existence of the electronic Church in America reveals that many find materialist society spiritually impoverished. It may also be showing that they find the established Churches unable to deal with that poverty. Critics rightly point out that electronic religion offers stones for bread, snakes for fish, and a 'presentation, gold-embossed Bible' for the Word of God. But many of those who are satisfied with stones, snakes and tacky gifts do not see the traditional Churches as offering anything at all.

4. A new dilemma

Religious broadcasts are not the only images of the Church that people receive through the media. Headlines such as 'Pulpit Poofs Can Stay', 'Who will Rid Me of this Turbulent Priest', 'A Flawed Gospel that is Beneath Contempt', stories about vicars running away with the organist, or cycling round the world, or bishops knitting their mitres is what happens when the news media tackle religion. Mainline Churches face a dilemma. If they try to influence *these* images (through press and publicity officers) then their attempts are subject to the same shaping and moulding pressures inherent in all news production (see chapter six). Like campaigning groups, trades unions and other minorities, they face almost overwhelming odds. If they attempt

to complement these news images through religious broadcasts over which they have more control, not only will
they soon have to face the huge costs of competing in a
commercial market, but they will also be subject to the
same pressures that televangelists currently face. The Christian message may hardly be recognisable in its electronic
proclamation.

The 1990 Broadcasting Act elicited two strands of Christian response. The mainline Churches and denominations,
with an eye to history and the experience of de-regulation
in America, Europe and Australia, supported a continued
ban on franchises being awarded to religious bodies. They
argued that, instead, religious broadcasts should be retained as part of a public service mix on the new commercial stations. Evangelical groups, however, argued that
if Messrs Murdoch and Maxwell were fit and right persons
to own a TV franchise, then Christian bodies were as well!
Churches should compete head on – with their own TV
stations broadcasting religious programmes as part of a
'family' output. (In the end, both were able to claim success!
The new commercial stations are obliged to carry religious
and children's programmes – and religious and Christian
groups will be able to own, run and control their own
cable and satellite stations.) It was not just a question of
different perspectives, different conceptions of the way
the media work, how to proclaim the Gospel and how
to respond to a new media environment. Behind the two
responses lay two very different notions of the Church,
its mission, its place in and its responsibility to society.

It may be comfortable and secure to retreat, like a sect,
into a narrowly defined religious ghetto, and devote one's
resources, energies and time to preaching largely to the
converted. But doing so abnegates a wider responsibility.
'The mere presence of a fundamentalist or neo-evangelical
message on television carries with it the implication that the
"dangerous", "debased", medium is being transformed.'[30]

In the face of these dilemmas, some advocate abandon-
ing the mass media altogether.[31] If they do that, though,

the Churches may well forfeit the only opportunities they have left to establish credible, alternative images in the public domain and offer a distinctly religious contribution to social debate. It may be costly to set up stall in tomorrow's commercial, electronic market place, but can they afford *not* to?

A Way Forward?

The dilemmas and problems with which religious broadcasting now confronts the Church may in part stem from its deeper failure to tackle more fundamental questions about the media and society. In 1975, an international study of the Churches' involvement with the media sounded a warning. It suggested that there was an unwillingness to address the structural and social issues which the mass media posed. It concluded that there was 'hardly any awareness of the seriousness of such items'.[32] The pressing need to get on with the job at hand had dulled a wider vision.

The fundamental question which underlies Church involvement with the media is not: How can the Church use the media? but, How should the media be structured to meet the needs of God's world? In sharing the myopic vision of those who have seen the media as a way of shaping, influencing or exercising power over society, the Church has failed to develop a much-needed critical edge. It needs to lend its support to attempts to create much more socially just, equitable and theologically appropriate models of communication which will allow all people their God-given right to communicate freely, to express their own hopes and aspirations and to have access to a wide range of views and opinions. Only when the media become sufficiently responsive to meet and reflect men and women's deepest needs will a Church committed to the same ends be at home within them. Dr Fore sums up what he sees as the Churches' failure: 'to treat communication in the Church as if it were public relations is both faulty theology and inept administration.'[33]

Perhaps a more exciting and theologically appropriate future for Church communications lies with the development of new, radical, popular, participatory community media which express new communication models rather than falling under the seductive spell of the new technologies of the computer age which currently serve a social system whose values are often in direct opposition to those of the Gospel.

Chapter Eight

Freedom or Captivity

'In questioning the ethics of mass communication, as in all questioning of the social order, the Churches dare not strike a self-righteous pose. They are deeply involved in every social process. Neither can the Churches derive benefit from something for which they will not assume responsibility. They cannot in conscience make widespread use of television, as they do, without assuming a large share of the burden of struggle to employ it in the interest of all of the people all of the time.'

E. C. Parker[1]

In October 1989, more than 450 Christians from 80 countries working in the field of communications met in the Philippines in Manila at the first world congress of the World Association for Christian Communication. They shared their concerns about the state of communications and people's rights and tried to set a common agenda for global communications issues.[2]

Their main conclusions were reflected in a conference declaration. First, that communication, one of God's gifts for humankind, should serve society as a whole and not be manipulated by a few or 'misappropriated by a single centre of power'.

Second, acknowledging an 'imbalance' in the state of communication (described at length in the UN MacBride Report), they called on Christians to work with others to 'achieve a common understanding of communication in the service of free, just and peaceful communities at the local and national levels'. An important guiding principle was to make the media much more accessible to ordinary people – to reflect their values, hopes and concerns.

The declaration went on to call on Churches and other groups to set a lead – 'to democratise their own media' and give priority to media that ordinary people can control and through which they could speak. The congress highlighted the potential of alternative, local and community-based communications initiatives to achieve that – and called on Christian communities to support them. It also asked them to take a lead in 'media awareness' training as a means of 'de-mystifying' the media.

The congress set an ambitious and sweeping agenda. It went well beyond the traditional concerns that Christians usually raise in connection with the media. Although far from exhaustive, the Manila declaration illustrates one aspect of critical media study. Just as the media cannot themselves be isolated, so their influence and effects, the problems they raise and the issues they throw up cannot be treated in isolation either. They are often symptoms of much deeper, underlying social concerns.

Here Might Be the News . . .

A study of news images, for example, goes far beyond a simple account of what we see on our screens or read in our papers. In a revolution, newspapers, radio and TV stations are often the first things to be seized. Radio broadcasts, wall newspapers and loudspeaker relays in remote villages were used to mobilise popular support for the people's revolution in China. In the Philippines, community media and Church-controlled radio stations, played their part in the largely peaceful overthrow of the Marcos dictatorship.[3] In the modern world, those who control the media use them to exercise immense ideological power.

Although the media occasionally provide examples of their potential to challenge the abuse of power, they are usually organised to reflect, endorse and enhance the position of those who hold power. In their struggle to preserve white domination and power in the 'eighties, the South African government exercised strict control over the media. In many totalitarian states, the media have become simply a government department. In liberal democracies, legislation, the courts, economic advantage and other informal 'controls' allow governments and powerful élites to exercise considerable influence.

Where power is used to perpetuate injustice, inequality and disadvantage, the Gospel demands that we stand alongside its victims, rather than its perpetrators. ' . . . We are sent to proclaim in word and deed, the good news of this new order of life *in* the multitudinous structures of society – family and government, business and neighbourhood, religion and education etc. In doing so we must stand, as Christ did, in solidarity with the poor and oppressed. Further, we must engage actively in their struggle for life and fulfilment.'[4] To 'family, government, business, neighbourhood, religion and education' we must surely add 'the media'. This 'active Christian engagement' will be exercised in two spheres: alongside those who are 'labelled', 'abused' and discriminated against by the media (even if we do not share their point of view) – marginal social groups, blacks, homosexuals, trade unions, women, etc; and in the very media systems which perpetuate and maintain injustice and the abuse of power – the control of technology and production for private commercial gain and advantage, the restricted access of disadvantaged groups and nations to channels of communication etc.

TV Religion

In developing Christian broadcasts we need to look beyond simple pragmatism – beyond what works and base our practice more fully on Biblical principles and sound practice. Unlike advertisers, we are not selling a commodity or trying to create dependent consumers. Rather the opposite, we are offering people freedom and independence. The forms of communication that we use need to reflect the substance of our message. For example, television formats and genres which are guaranteed to 'grab an audience' or elicit an emotional response are certainly part of our communications environment. They will undoubtedly be part of the repertoire of the Christian communicator. But as many American televangelists have shown, in a broadcast system which measures effectiveness purely in the numbers who 'switch on' and the money raised, they can effectively eclipse the light of the Gospel in Christian programming. The cult of the 'media personality' may be an effective way to arouse interest and sell magazines, but it does little to help Christian readers understand that all are equal in God's sight.

The 1990 Broadcasting Act, with new obligations for commercial broadcasters to transmit 'religious' programmes and new opportunities for Christian and religious bodies to own TV and radio stations and advertise freely on the media, means that Christians in Britain will have to face these issues sooner rather than later.

Horsfield's description of religious programmes produced in a competitive television environment – authoritative, individualistic, materialistic and paradoxical (see p. 112) is quite alarming.

Some feel that given proper safeguards and legislation to prevent groups appealing for funds on air, British religious broadcasts will be different. They point to a long history of responsible and creative programmes. Besides, they argue, Britain is not America. These are not features of *competitive* TV religion, but *American* TV religion.

Others are more circumspect. They point to the fact that although the medium may not be the message, *per se*, form and content are not so easily disentangled. Any proclamation of the Gospel is partial and incomplete. There may be elements of the Christian message which are authoritative, which appeal to the individual, which touch the material world and which present people with a paradox – but they are only part of the Gospel. The danger is not that British TV religion will be an exact replica of US religion (although many think it likely) but that the equivalent (if not identical) commercial forces which will mould and shape de-regulated British television will render TV religion just as partial and incomplete. That will be less of a danger to those within the Church, who have other means of testing and complementing their message, than those for whom TV religion is their main, if fleeting, point of contact.

A Word from our Sponsors

Advertising doesn't just raise questions about the range and content of today's media, the dominance of consumer values raises much more fundamental questions about society and the way we see ourselves. Production, marketability, consumption technique and scientific method are not evil in themselves and have, in fact, bestowed great benefits on humanity. But some critics claim that a right relationship with them has been reversed. The 'instrumentals' of modern society have become the measure of the person.

Although there are other instances of idolatory besides consumerism – the collective state, the bureaucratic Church, the institutionalisation of the personality cult, for example – nevertheless, in the final decade of the twentieth century our TV screens show pictures of East Berliners streaming enviously towards the bright lights and gaudy consumer displays of western Europe. It is the values of the games shows, the advertisements and the soap operas that the media are spreading around the world.

In his devastating critique of what he calls 'the commodity form' Kavanaugh suggests that the values of consumer society extend to the way we see ourselves. 'Possessions which might otherwise serve as *expressions* of our humanity, and enhance us as persons, are transformed into ultimates. Our being is in having. Our happiness is said to be in possessing more. Our drive to consume, bolstered by an economics of infinite growth, becomes addictive: it moves from manipulated need, to the promise of joy in things, to broken promises and frustrated expectation, to guilt and greater need for buying. Property is no longer instrumental to our lives; it is the final judge of our merit.'[5]

Even sexuality – 'the embodied expression of our person-hood'[6] – is marketed and becomes a battleground for competition, a stage for aggression and self-infatuation. Marketing has become an end – not a means. Its values are reinforced, legitimised and fostered by the advertising industry's economic and ideological dominance of the media. 'The commodification of the human person is relentless and omnipresent,' comments Kavanaugh.[7]

In the process, Christian values such as faith, hope, love and even freedom are devalued – their reputation in purely material terms effectively emptying them of any deeper meaning. 'It is important to realise that the very nature of our economic system provides a faith challenge for those who wish to live the Christian life. In an economic world which is based upon continually expanding consumption, in a society which already has a super-abundance of goods and services, in a society which makes consumption, marketing and producing such absolute values, there are questions that must be raised. What kind of person is *most suitable* for such an economic system? What kind of person, what kind of behaviour is *least desirable*?'[8]

The whole commodity form – promoted and promulgated and exemplified through consumer advertising – is idolatrous, creating impersonal idols which in turn depersonalise us. It stands in direct opposition to the 'personal' form of human existence revealed in Jesus Christ.

The Rambo Syndrome?

Tom Davies's colourful and highly readable account of the influence of media violence purports to be undeniable 'well documented fact'.[9] Unfortunately, firm assertion is no substitute for hard evidence. A *very* few films, such as *Rambo*, and books, such as *Catcher in the Rye*, are often cited as being responsible for horrific and tragic examples of criminal behaviour. However, the very regularity with which the same few books and films are blamed is evidence of their lack of culpability. If the media were the powerful and persuasive determinants of deviant behaviour, as many claim, then there would be many more examples that could be cited, and Japan – with possibly the most violent television in the world – would be awash with such crimes.

The complex relationship between the media and violent behaviour raises much more fundamental questions than the direct influence of violent screen images. Those who constantly reassert and reaffirm a narrow, direct behavioural relationship are under some obligation to take seriously the results of much conflicting detailed research and the genuine claims of those who conclude that this influence is, in fact, negligible. A wider concern demands that we look much more closely at the circumstances in which violence is perpetuated, condoned and even legitimised, in society and the specific and general contributions that the media make to them.

Just as the media themselves open our eyes to the wider world of which they are a part, so a concern for the way in which they are used and the effect they have on the lives of their viewers, listeners and readers opens our eyes to a wider range of social, political and economic issues – of which they are variously both a symptom and a cause.

Christians have long since recognised a need to concern themselves with the moral issues posed by nuclear weapons, apartheid, war, human sexuality, political and economic injustice. They have, by and large, failed to develop an equivalent, informed response to one of the outstanding and pervasive features of modern society – the mass media.

Taking Control

In his book *Super Media*, Michael Real argues that media consumers need to win back control over their media. He outlines ways in which viewers and listeners can become more active and unlock the liberating potential of the media.

First, by sharing and controlling their use of the media. Parents are encouraged to take an interest in the media their children consume – by talking to them about the books they read, the films they've been to, by watching TV with them and helping them interpret the experience. The media's interpretation of events can be discussed and shared. Without a reference group, a lone individual can become immensely more susceptible to misrepresentations, fads and superficiality. An interpretive community – peers, parents, critics, friends, or a church group can become a useful reference point. Simply finding a group of people who can talk critically about what they have seen, heard or read can raise awareness of how important the media have become.

Second, by using the media to stimulate responsibility and growth. There are times when we need just to flop in a chair and listen to our favourite record or watch mindless drivel, or skim through a trivial magazine. But although most people tune into the media for entertainment – they are just as appreciative of its potential to 'educate and inform'. It is not just good for society that programmes such as *Panorama*, *Newsnight* and *TV Eye* are available, that *The Times* and *Guardian* are on sale alongside the *Sun* and the *Mirror*, that BBC-speech-based local radio is available alongside ILR music stations. Life is more than food and clothes. We need to work as much at caring for our media environment as we are beginning to do for our natural one – and make sure that from it we can get a balanced, healthy, media diet.

But we can only choose from what is available. That is one reason why Church groups in Britain and Europe have been so concerned to support the principle of public service broadcasting and why Christians have joined others in protest groups such as the Campaign for Press and Broadcasting Freedom.

Third, by working to 'democratise' the media. Media professionals and executives are much more adept at making TV programmes or running commercial organisations which conform to commercial imperatives or constraints than in developing media which are more accountable and serve the public interest. 'This requiries an effort to find or create alternative media, to organise for positive change, to influence media policies, regulations, and practices. From making programming for local cable access to lobbying regulators, one must produce as well as consume, act as well as react if our media are to become what they might be.'[10]

All this requires real effort. It is not easy to move from being a passive recipient to an active participant. To become knowledgeable participants in the media world requires time, energy, ideas, criticism and questioning – the classical components of what some have called 'active citizens'. And, as Kavanaugh points out, it means working against the very values, motives and mores that the media perpetuate. But it is the only course open to us if we are to take our Christian responsibility seriously and join with others in the attempt to create and liberate the media in the service of humankind.

Throughout the centuries, the Church has proclaimed the liberating and life-giving Good News of Jesus Christ. We are called to do so today. We have now more communication opportunities than ever before to tell men and women that they can be free from all that binds them and holds them captive in the twentieth century. But we also need to discover and proclaim what it means for them to be freed from captivity to and captivation by those same communications media.

End Notes

Chapter One

1. *Church of England Newspaper*, 10th May, 1990
2. Morris, C., 1984, p.14
3. Gerbner, G., 'A New Environmental Movement on Communication and Culture,' in *Media Development*, April 1990, p. 13ff.
4. Matt. 25:40
5. Real, M., 1989, p.250

Chapter Two

1. Ball-Rokeach, S. J. & Cantor, M. G. (eds.), 1986, p.11
2. Golding, P., 1974, p.78
3. Hamelink, C., 1975, p.61
4. Most of the BBC's research findings fall into these categories (e.g., *see* annual Review of BBC Research Findings No. 12, 1986)
5. Himmelweitt, H. *et al*, 1958
6. Barlow, G. & Hill, A. (eds.), 1985
7. They were, however, largely the product of exaggeration by other media, *see* McQuail, D., 1977, p.86
8. McQuail, D., 1977
9. Cumberbatch, B. & Howitt, D., 1989

10. General Synod of the Church of England, Report of Proceedings, 21st February, 1990 p. 246
11. Harrison, M., 1985, and review by Howard Davis in 'Third Way', March, 1987
12. Golding, P., 1974, p.1

Chapter Three

1. Ball-Rokeach, S. J., & Cantor, M. G., p.19
2. James, Clive, 1981, p.19
3. Gitlin, T., 1980, p.1
4. Barlow, G., & Hill, A., 1985, p.121
5. *see* articles by O'Donnell & O'Donnell, J. Maracek *et al*, & Denise Warren in 'What Does "She" Mean', *Journal of Communication*, Vol. 128, Winter 1978, pp.156 ff.
6. Knott, K., 1984
7. Glasgow University Media Group, 1982
8. Morley, D., 1980
9. *see* C. Brunsdon, 1981, pp.32–7
10. IBA Research Dept, 1986 (approx)
11. Tunstall, J. 1983, pp.161–5
12. *see* R. H. Turner & D. H. Paz, 'Mass Media in Earthquake Warning', and P. L. Hirshburg, D. A. Dillman & S. J. Ball-Rokeach, 'Media System Dependency Theory' in Ball-Rokeach & Cantor, 1986
13. Fore, W., 1987, p.67
14. Hartmann, P., Husband C. & Clark, J., 'Race as News: a study in the handling of race in the British national press', in J. D. Halloran (ed.), 1974
15. Murdock, G. & Golding, P., 'Capitalism, Communication and Class Relations' in Curran *et al*, 1977, pp.23–33
16. Burns, T., 'The Organisation of Public Opinion' in Curran *et al*, 1977, p.67
17. *see* S. MacBride, 1980. Countries such as Britain and America (in whose economic and ideological interest the concept of a 'free' flow largely operated) objected and eventually withdrew from UNESCO

18. Syvertsen, T., 1987, p.31
19. Postman, N., 1986
20. Golding, P., & Murdock, G., 'Communications Technologies and Public Interest' in Ferguson, M.H. (ed.), 1986, p.76
21. Schiller, H., 'Information for What Kind of Society' in Salvaggio, J. (ed.), 1983, p.28
22. Golding, P., 1974, p.85

Chapter Four

1. Whitehouse, M., 1977, p.15
2. Halloran, J. D., 1978, p.827
3. Fore, W., 1987, p.144
4. Wyatt Committee, BBC 1987 (a)
5. Barlow, G. & Hill, A. (eds.), 1985, p.168
6. Kaplan, R. M. & Singer, R. D., 1976, pp.36 & 64
7. *see* BBC, 1987(a) and BBC, 1987(b)
8. *see* 'Britain to Control TV Violence' *Action* (World Association for Christian Communication Newsletter), October, 1987, No.119, p.1
9. Brown, D., 'Bitter Controversy over TV Violence', *Church Times*, 2.10.87
10. An informal group of parliamentarians and Churchmen set up in July, 1983, 'to produce factual evidence relating to the effects upon children of their viewing scenes of violence in video films'.
11. Whitehouse, M., 1977, p.15
12. Surgeon General's Advisory Committee on Television and Social Behavior, 1972, p.7
13. *see* Rubinstein, E. A., 1976, and Kaplan, R. M. & Singer, R. D., 1976
14. *see* Fore W., 1987, chapter eight, 'Media Violence is Hazardous to Your Health'
15. *see* Melville-Davis G., in G. Barlow and A. Hill, 1985, p.14
16. Belson, W., 1978, p.393

17. Belson, W., 1978 & Milavsky, J. R. etc, 1982
18. *see* Murdock, G., & McCron, R., 1979, pp.51–67
19. Barlow, G. & Hill, A., (eds) 1985
20. McClure, J. M., 1981
21. *see* e.g., Rice, R. E. & Paisley, W. J. (eds), 1981
22. Bettelheim, B., 1990, p.151
23. Even Melville-Davis, who has argued strongly in support of tighter censorship, after reviewing the evidence concludes that 'despite many studies' emphasis on the association between exposure to violence and behaviour none has so-far been able to provide unequivocal proof of causality.' Barlow G. & Hill A., 1985, p.20
24. IBA, 1986, p.5ff.
25. 'The News' is the programme mentioned most often in the letters the BBC receives complaining about violence. *see* BBC, 1987(a), p.9
26. Galtung, J., 1986
27. Halloran, J. D., *et al*, 1970, p.315
28. Hall, S., *et al*, 1978, p.221
29. Pietilä, Veikko, 1976
30. Gerbner, G., 1986
31. *Ibid*.
32. Archbishop of Canterbury's Commission on Urban Priority Areas, 1985: *'Faith in the City'*
33. McClure, J. M., 1981, p.353
34. *see* Halloran, J., 1978, pp.816–33. In spite of their claim to have extensively examined the effects of media violence on the viewer, the Parliamentary Video Group's report 'Video, Violence & Children' ignored this important relationship

Chapter Five

1. Postman, N., 1986, p.126
2. IBA Yearbook, 1987, p.160
3. Schultze, Q. J., 1987, p.2
4. *Media Development*, 1987/3, p.1

5. Postman, N., 1986, p.130
6. Murdock, G., & Janus, N., 1985, Table 27, p.60; Table 28, p.61
7. IBA 1986 (a); IBA 1986 (b); BBC 1986
8. *Media Development*, 1987/3
9. Henry, B., 1986
10. Myers, K., 1986, p.49
11. Dyer, G., 1982, p.79
12. *Ibid.*, p.9
13. Myers, K., 1986, p.51
14. Williamson, J., 1978, p.31
15. Berman, R., 1981, p.105
16. Schultze, Q. J., 1987, p.3
17. Williams, R., 1980, p.185
18. Real, M., 1989, p.254
19. Jenkins, D., 1970, p.75
20. Wolff, H. W., 1974, p.226
21. Berman, R., 1981, p.102
22. Kavanaugh, J. F., 1986, p.26
23. Real, M., 1989, p.254
24. Millum, T., 1975, p.181
25. Warren, D., 1978, p.169
26. Halloran, J., 1978
27. Henry, B., 1986, p.15
28. Murdock, G. & Janus, N., 1985, p.58
29. Wilson, T., in K. Myers, 1986, p.115
30. Myers, K., 1987, p.13
31. Curran, J., 1981, p.229
32. Royal Commission on the Press, 1977:105
33. Hird, P., 1981, p.6, quoted in G. Murdock & N. Janus, op. cit.
34. Myers, K., 1986, p.115
35. *see* Curran, J., 1978
36. Curran, J., 1981
37. Tunstall, J., 1971
38. Curran, J., 1978
39. In 1987, the *Daily Star* attempted to compete with its rival the *Sun* by being even more raunchy and brash.

Market research showed, however, that its new style appealed to low-income, low-spending groups. This led to the withdrawal of support by a number of major consumer advertisers. The paper responded by attempting to adjust its image, and restore its appeal amongst women and higher spenders to win back its advertising support.

40. Murdock, G., & Janus, N., op.cit., p.61
41. Seaton, J., 1978, p.307
42. Dyer, G., 1982, p.61
43. Institute of Practitioners of Advertising, 1982
44. Murdock, G., 1982(b), p.145
45. Beloff, N., 1976, p.14
46. Murdock, G. & Janus, N., op.cit., p.12
47. Fore, W., 1987, p.188

Chapter Six

1. Golding, P. & Elliott, P., 1979, p.151
2. White, R. A., 1980
3. Jackson, H., 1978, p.200
4. Glasgow University Media Group, 1982, p.16
5. Matta, F., 1987, p.13
6. *Church Times*, 13.11.87, p.22
7. Glasgow University Media Group, 1982, p.1
8. Nichols, D., CBE, editor and chief executive of ITN
9. *see* Bush, R., 1985, *Marxism Today*, December, 1985, pp.8–11
10. White, R. A., 1980, p.11
11. Christian, H., (in Christian, H. (ed.), 1980) argues that this professional ideology arose in part as a reaction by journalists whose work was primarily to enhance the financial and political objectives of the newspaper proprietors.
12. Chibnall, S., 1977
13. Glasgow University Media Group, 1982; 1985
14. Golding, P., & Middleton, S., 1982, p.124

15. Elliott, P., 1978, p.147
16. Golding, P., & Middleton, S., 1982, p.152
17. Golding, P., & Elliott, P., 1979, p.151
18. *see* Cohen's (1972) analysis of the Mods/Rockers reporting
19. Hall, S., *et al*, 1978, p.79
20. Golding, P., & Middleton, S., 1982, p.128
21. Murdock, G., 1974, quoted in S. Hall (*et al*), 1978, p.56
22. Field, M., 1987
23. *see* Knott, K., 1984; Buchstein, F. D., 1972; Shaw, D., 1985
24. Golding, P., & Middleton, S., p.152
25. Johnstone, J. W., 1976, p.185
26. *see* e.g., Rainly, D., 1979
27. Gallagher, M., 1984, p.4
28. Golding, P., & Elliott, P., 1979
29. Schlessinger, P., 1978, p.47
30. Tremayne, C. T., 1980
31. Golding, P., & Elliott, P., 1979, p.71ff.
32. Tunstall, J., 1971
33. Golding, P., & Elliott, P., 1979, p.137. *See also* S. Chibnall, 1977, p.113; J. D. Halloran, 1974, p.17
34. Fishmann, M., 1980, p.51. This is supported in part by H. J. Gans, 1979, p.124 who notes similarities in position, age, race and other characteristics between journalists and their sources.
35. Golding, P. & Middleton, S., p.149
36. *see* Field, M., 1987
37. Cockerell, M., *et al*, 1984, p.233
38. Chibnall, S., 1977, illustrates this in the case of information 'embargoed' or falsely released by the police in the public interest, although he notes that the definition of 'public interest' is supplied by the police and only operates by collusion from journalists.
39. Morley, D., 1976, p.255
40. Real, M., 1989, p.251
41. Glasgow University Media Group, 1982, p.168

Chapter Seven

1. Hoover, S., in F. P. Frost (ed.), 1982
2. Elvy, P., 1986, p.139
3. White, R. A., 1983, p.9
4. Morris, C., 1984, p.230
5. Reith, J., 1924, p.200
6. Knott, K., 1984
7. Elvy, P., 1986, p.144
8. *Crockfords Clerical Directory*, 1987
9. Gans, H. J., 1979, p.124
10. Harris, B. F., 1980, Vol.2, p.953
11. Falconer, R., 1977
12. *see* Field, M., 1988
13. Knott, K., 1984, p.69
14. Elvy, P., 1986, p.142
15. Hadden, J., & Swann C., 1981, p.13
16. Chapter title from government green paper, 'Radio: Choices and Opportunities', Command Paper 92, HMSO, February, 1987
17. *Media Development*, 1985/2, p.1
18. Hoover, S., 1982
19. Morris, C., 1984
20. Elvy, P., 1986
21. *see* Field, M., 1988, *op.cit.*
22. *see* Horsfield, P., 1984
23. Hoover, S., 1988, p.221
24. Owens, Virginia Stem, 1980, p.52
25. Fore, W., 1987, chapter six
26. quoted in Fore, W., 1987, p.109
27. *Ibid.*
28. Stacey, W., & Shupe, A., 1982
29. Hoover, S., 1988, p.224
30. Loving, Rev. J. H., Grace Episcopal Church, Oklahoma. Quoted in T. Cardwell, 1984
31. *see* Owens, V. S., 1980
32. Hamelink, C., 1975, p.129

33. Fore, W., 1987, p.196

Chapter Eight

1. Parker, E. C., 1961
2. 'Communication and Community. The Manila Declaration,' October, 1989, WACC, London
3. Dionisio, E. R., 1986, 'Small Media, Big Victory' & Murphy, D., 1986, 'Church Media Play a Vital Role' in *Media Development*, 1986/4
4. Costas, Orlando. E., 1974, p.93
5. Kavanaugh, J. F., 1986, p.42
6. *Ibid.*, p.43
7. *Ibid.*, p.46
8. *Ibid.*, p.46
9. Davies, T., 1989
10. Real, M., 1989, p.259

Bibliography

ARCHBISHOP OF CANTERBURY'S COMMISSION
ON URBAN PRIORITY AREAS, *Faith in the City*,
London, Church House Publishing, 1985

BALL-ROKEACH, S.J. & CANTOR, M.G. (eds), *Media,
Audience and Social Structure*, Beverly Hills &
London, Sage, 1986

BARLOW, G. & HILL, A. (eds), *Video, Violence and
Children*, London, Hodder & Stoughton, 1985

BELOFF, N. *Freedom Under Foot*, London, Maurice
Temple Smith, 1976

BELSON, W. *Television Violence and the Adolescent Boy*,
London, Saxon House, 1978

BERMAN, R. *Advertising and Social Change*, California,
Sage, 1981

BETTELHEIM, B., *Recollections and Reflections*, London,
Thames & Hudson, 1990

BRITISHBROADCASTINGCORPORATION,Broadcasting
Research Department, *Annual Review of BBC
Broadcasting Research Findings No.12*, 1986, London,
BBC Data Publications, 1986

BRITISH BROADCASTING CORPORATION, *Annual
Report & Handbook 1987*, London, BBC, 1986

BRITISH BROADCASTING CORPORATION, *Violence on
Television: the report of the Wyatt Committee*, London,
BBC, 1987(a)

BRITISH BROADCASTING CORPORATION, *Violence*

on Television: guidelines for production staff,
London, BBC, 1987(b)

BRUNSDON, C., ' "Crossroads": Notes on Soap Opera,'
Screen, Vol.22, 1981

BUCHSTEIN, F.D. 'The Role of the News Media in the
Death of God Controversy', *Journalism Quarterly,*
49(1), Spring, 1972

BUSH, R., in *Marxism Today,* Dec., 1985

CARDWELL, T., *Mass Media Christianity,* Lanham,
University Press of America, 1984

CHIBNALL, S., *Law and Order News,* London, Tavistock,
1977

CHRISTIAN, H. (ed.), The Sociology of Journalism and the
Press, *Sociological review,* Monograph 29, University of
Keele, 1980

COCKERELL, M., HENNESSY P., & WALKER
D., *Sources Close to the Prime Minister,* London,
Macmillan, 1984

COHEN, S., *Folk Devils and Moral Panics: the Creation
of the Mods and Rockers,* London, McGibbon
& Kee, 1972

COSTAS, O.E., *The Church and Its Mission: A Shattering
Critique from the Third World,* Wheaton, Illinois,
Tyndale, 1974

CUMBERBATCH, B. & HOWITT, D., *A Measure
of Uncertainty: the Effects of the Mass Media,*
Broadcasting Standards Council Research Monograph
Series: 1, London, John Libbey, 1989

CURRAN, J. (ed.) *The British Press: a Manifesto,* London,
Macmillan, 1978

CURRAN, J., 'The Impact of Advertising on the British
Mass Media' in *Media, Culture & Society* 1981/3, No.1,
Jan., pp.229–267

CURRAN, J., ECCLESTONE, J., OAKLEY, G., &
RICHARDSON, A. (eds.) *Bending Reality,* London,
Pluto, 1986

CURRAN, J., GUREVITCH, M. & WOOLLACOTT,
J., *Mass Communication and Society,* London,

Arnold/Open University Press, 1977

DAVIES, T., *The Man of Lawlessness*, London, Hodder & Stoughton, 1989

DOUGLAS, J.D., *Let the Earth Hear His Voice*, Minneapolis, World Wide Publications, 1975

DYER, G., *Advertising as Communication*, London, Methuen, 1982

ELLIOTT, P., 'All the World's a Stage', in CURRAN (ed.), 1978, *op. cit.*

ELVY, P., *Buying Time*, Gt. Wakering, McCrimmons, 1986

ENGEL, J.F., *Contemporary Christian Communications*, Nashville, Nelson, 1979

FALCONER, R., *Message, Media, Mission* (Baird Lectures 1975) Edinburgh, St Andrew Press, 1977

FERGUSON, M. (ed.), *New Communication Technologies and the Public Interest: comparative perspectives on policy and research*, London, Sage, 1986

FIELD, M., 'Faith in the City: a case study of religious news' in *Southwell and Oxford Papers on Church and Society*, September, 1987

FIELD, M., 'Here Today and Gone Tomorrow: the Future of Religious Broadcasting', *Modern Churchman*, June 1988

FISHMANN, M., *Manufacturing the News*, Austin, University of Texas Press, 1980

FORE, W., *Television and Religion*, Minneapolis, Augsburg, 1987

FROST, F.P. (ed.), *A Vision All Can Share*, US Catholic conference, Department of Communication, 1982

GALLAGHER, M., 'Parallels and Paradoxes of Women and the NWICO', *Media Development*, Vol. XXXI, 1984/2, pp.2–6, WACC

GALTUNG, J., 'Social Communication and Global Problems' in LEE, P. (ed.), *Communication For All* New York, Orbis Books, 1986

GANS, H.J., *Deciding What's News*, New York, Pantheon, 1979

GENERAL SYNOD OF THE CHURCH OF ENGLAND,

Report of Proceedings, Vol.21, No.1, General Synod, February Group of Sessions 1990, London, General Synod of the Church of England, 1990

GERBNER, G., *(et al)*, *Recent Developments in Culture Indictors: Violence Profile No. 14–15 and the Social Role of TV Violence* (unpublished) monograph of University of Pennsylvania, 1986

GITLIN, T., *The Whole World is Watching*, California & London, University of California Press, 1980

GLASGOW UNIVERSITY MEDIA GROUP, *Really Bad News*, London, Writers and Readers Pub., 1982

GLASGOW UNIVERSITY MEDIA GROUP, *War News, Peace News*, London, Open University Press, 1985

GOLDING, P., *The Mass Media*, Harlow, Longman, 1974

GOLDING, P. & ELLIOTT, P. *Making the News*, London, Longman, 1979

GOLDING, P. & MIDDLETON, S., *Images of Welfare*, Oxford, Robertson, 1982

GUREVITCH, M., BENNETT, T., CURRAN, J., & WOOLLACOTT, J., (eds.), *Culture, Society and the Media*, London, Methuen, 1982

HADDEN, J. & SWANN, C., *Prime Time Preachers: the rising power of tele-evangelism*, Reading (Mass), Addison Wesley, 1981

HALL, S. *(et al)*, *Policing the Crisis – Mugging, the State and the Law*, London, Macmillan, 1978

HALLORAN, J.D., *The Effects of Television*, London, Panther, 1970

HALLORAN, J.D., 'Mass Media and Race: a research approach', in *Race as News*, UNESCO, Paris, 1974

HALLORAN, J., 'Mass Communications: symptom or cause of violence?', *International Social Science Journal*, 30/4, pp.816–33, 1978

HALLORAN, J. ELLIOTT P. & MURDOCK, G., *Demonstrations and Communication: a case study*, Harmondsworth, Penguin Books, 1970

HAMELINK, C., *Perspectives for Public Communication:*

a study of the Churches' participation in public communication, Baarn, Ten Have, 1975

HARRIS, B.F., *The Illustrated Bible Dictionary*, Leicester, IVP, 1980

HARRISON, M., *TV News: Whose Bias?*, London, Policy Journals, 1985

HENRY, B., *British Television Advertising*, London, Century Benham, 1986

HIMMELWEITT, H., OPPENHEIM, A.N., & VINCE, P., *Television And The Child*, London, Oxford University Press/Nuffield Foundation, 1958

HOOVER, S., *The Electronic Giant*, Elgin, Brethren Press, 1982

HOOVER, S., *Mass Media Religion*, London, Sage, 1988

HORSFIELD, P., *Religious Television: the American experience*, New York, Longman, 1984

INDEPENDENT BROADCASTING AUTHORITY 1986 (a), *Television and Radio 1987*, London, IBA

INDEPENDENT BROADCASTING AUTHORITY, *Annual Report and Accounts 1985/6*, London, IBA, 1986(b)

INDEPENDENT BROADCASTING AUTHORITY RESEARCH DEPARTMENT, *Attitudes to Broadcasting*, London, IBA, 1986(c)

INSTITUTE OF THE PRACTITIONERS OF ADVERTISING, *Submission to the Inquiry into Cable Expansion and Broadcasting Policy*, London, IPA, 1982

JACKSON, H., 'The Making of Foreign News' in CURRAN, J., (ed.), 1978, *op. cit.*

JAMES, C., *The Crystal Bucket*, London, Jonathan Cape, 1981

JENKINS, D., *What is Man?*, London, SCM, 1970

JOHNSTONE J.W., *The News People*, London, University of Illinois Press, 1976

KAPLAN, E. (ed.), *Regarding Television: critical approaches – an anthology*, American Film Institute Monograph Vol.2, California University Publications of America Inc., 1983

KAPLAN, R.M. & SINGER, R.D., 'Television Violence

and Viewer Aggression: a re-examination of the
evidence' in *Journal of Social Issues* 32/4, pp.18–70,
November, 1976

KAVANAUGH, J.F., *Following Christ in a Consumer
Society*, New York, Orbis, 1986

KENNEDY, G.S., *The Word and the Work*, London,
Longmans Green, 1925

KNOTT, K., *Media Portrayals of Religion and their
Reception*, final report sponsored by Christendom
Trust, University of Leeds, unpublished, 1984

LANG, K. & LANG, G.E., 'The Unique Perspective
of Television and Its Effect: a Pilot Study', in
SCHRAMM, W. (ed.), *Mass Communication*,
University of Illinois Press, 1960

LONGLEY, C., *The End of a Road*, IBA Religious
Consultation (unpublished), 1983

MacBRIDE, S., *Many Voices, One World*, Paris & London,
UNESCO & Kogan Page, 1980

McCLURE, J.M., *Spike Island – Portrait of a Police
Division*, London, Pan Books, 1981

McDONNEL, J. & TRAMPETS, F., *Communicating Faith
in a Technological Age*, Middlegreen, St Paul, 1989

McQUAIL, D., 'The Influence and Effects of Mass
Media' in CURRAN, J., GUREVITCH, M., &
WOOLLACOTT, J., 1977, *op. cit.*

MATTA, F.R.A., 'Latin American Journalism: new avenues
towards democratisation', in *Media Development* 1987/4
WACC, pp.12–14, 1987

MILAVSKY, J.R. etc. *Television and Aggression: a panel
study*, New York, Academic Press, 1982

MILLUM, T., *Images of Woman*, London, Chatto &
Windus, 1975

MORLEY, D., 'Industrial Conflict and the Mass Media' in
The Sociological Review, Vol. 24, No.2, 1976

MORLEY, D., *The Nationwide Audience*, TV Monograph
11, London, BFI, 1980

MORRIS, C., *God in a Box*, London, Hodder & Stoughton,
1984

MORRIS, C., 'Love at a Distance – the Spiritual Challenges
    of Religious Broadcasting' in *Media Development*,
    1986/4, WACC, pp. 40–1, 1986
MUGGERIDGE, M., *Christ and the Media*, London,
    Hodder & Stoughton, 1977
MURDOCK, G., (a) *'Mass Communication and Social
    Violence: a critical review of recent research trends'*,
    in Marsh & Campbell (eds.), *Aggression and Violence*,
    pp.62–90, Oxford, Blackwell, 1982(a)
MURDOCK, G., (b) 'Large Corporations and the Control
    of the Communications Industries', in GUREVITCH,
    BENNETT, CURRAN & WOOLLACOTT (eds.),
    chapter five. *op. cit.*, 1982(b)
MURDOCK, G. & JANUS, N., *Mass Communications and
    the Advertising Industry*: *Reports and Papers on Mass
    Communications, No. 97* Paris, UNESCO, 1985
MURDOCK, G. & McCRON, R., 'The Television and
    Delinquency Debate', *Screen Education*, Spring,
    1979, p.51–67
MYERS, K., *Understains: The Sense and Seduction of
    Advertising*, London, Comedia, 1986
MYERS, K. 'Advertising Strategies Snare the Unwary', in
    Media Development, 1987/3, WACC
NATIONAL COMMISSION ON THE CAUSES AND
    PREVENTION OF VIOLENCE, *Final Report*, USA
    Government Printing Office, 1969
OWENS, V.S., *The Total Image*, Grand Rapids, W.B.
    Eerdmans, 1980
PARKER, E.C., *Religious Television*, New York, Harper,
    1961
PIETILÄ, V., 'Notes on Violence in the Mass Media' in
    Instant Research on Peace and Violence, Tampere
    Peace Research Institute, Finland No.4, 1976
POSTMAN, N., *Amusing Ourselves to Death*, London,
    Heinemann, 1986
RAINLY, D., 'How do Religious Editors of Newspapers
    View their Jobs and Religion', *Journalism Quarterly*
    56(4), Winter, 1979

REAL, M., *Super Media*, London, Sage, 1989

REITH, J., *Broadcast Over Britain*, London, Hodder & Stoughton, 1924

RICE, R.E. & PAISLEY, W.J. (eds.), *Public Communications Campaigns*, Beverley Hills, Sage, 1981

ROYAL COMMISSION ON THE PRESS, *Final Report*, Her Majesty's Stationery Office, Cmnd 6810–1, 1977

RUBINSTEIN, E.A., 'Warning: The Surgeon General's Program May Be Dangerous to Preconceived Notions' in *Journal of Social Issues* 32/4, pp.18–70, November, 1976

SALVAGGIO, J. (ed.), *Telecommunications: Issues and Choices for Society*, New York & London, Longman, 1983

SCHLESSINGER, P., *Putting Reality Together: BBC News*, London, Constable, 1978

SCHULTZE, Q.J., 'Poets For Hire: the ethics of consumer advertising' in *Media Development*, 1987/3, WACC

SEATON, J., 'Government Policy and the Mass Media' in CURRAN (ed.), 1978, *op. cit.*

SHAW, D., 'Media View Religion in a News Light' in ELDON & REUSS (eds.), *Impact of Mass Media*, New York, Longman, 1985

SOUKUP, P., *Communication and Theology*, London, WACC, 1983

STACEY, W. & SHUPE, A., 'Correlates of Support for the Electronic Church' in *Journal for the Scientific Study of Religion*, 21(4) pp.291–303, 1982

SUGDEN, C., *Radical Discipleship*, London, Marshalls, 1981

SURGEON GENERAL'S ADVISORY COMMITTEE ON TELEVISION AND SOCIAL BEHAVIOR, *Television and Growing up: The Impact of Televised Violence: Report to the Surgeon General* (United States Public Health Service), US Department of Health, Education and Welfare, 1972

SYVERTSEN, T., *Ny Teknikk, Ny Politikk Og «Nye» Medier*, Rapport No.4, Institutt for Massekommunikasjon, Bergen, Norway, 1987

TILLICH, P., *Morality and Beyond*, London, Routledge & Kegan Paul, 1964

TREMAYNE, C.T., 'The Social Organisation of Newspaper Houses' in CHRISTIAN, H. (ed.), 1980, *op. cit.*

TUNSTALL, J., *Journalists at Work*, London, Constable, 1971

TUNSTALL, J., *The Media in Britain*, London, Constable, 1983

WARREN, D., 'What Does "She" Mean? Commercial Liberation' in *Journal of Communication*, Vol.28, pp.169–173, Winter, 1978

WHITE, R.A., 'The Contribution of Research to News Reform', *Communication Research Trends*, Vol. 1, No.4, Winter, 1980

WHITE, R.A., 'The Growing Dialogue between Theology and Communications', in SOUKUP, 1983, *op. cit.*

WHITE, R.E.O., *The Changing Continuity of Christian Ethics: Vol.2 The Insights of History*, Exeter, Paternoster, 1981

WHITEHOUSE, M. *Whatever Happened to Sex?* London, Hodder & Stoughton, 1977

WILLIAMS, R., 'Advertising: the magic system', in *Problems in Materialism and Culture*, Ch.4 pp.170–195, London, Verso, 1980

WILLIAMS, R., *Television: Technology and Cultural Form*, London, Fontana, 1974

WILLIAMSON, J., *Decoding Advertisements*, London, Marion Boyars, 1978

WOLFE, K.M., *The Churches and the British Broadcasting Corporation 1922–1956*, London, SCM, 1984

WOLFF, H.W., *Anthropology of the Old Testament*, London, SCM, 1974